Girls' Life

Guide to Being the Most AMAZING YOU

From the creators of *Girls' Life magazine*

Edited by Sarah Wassner Flynn

Scholastic Inc.

New York   Toronto   London   Auckland
Sydney   Mexico City   New Delhi   Hong Kong

All of the awesome advice and info in this book would've been impossible to provide without the fabulous staff of *Girls' Life* as well as these oh-so-wise writers: Abby Brunson, Jodi Bryson, Kate Callahan, Sandy Fertman Ryan, Mandy Forr, Lisa Mulcahy, Jennifer Pangyanszki, Laura Purdie Salas, Robin VanTan, and Michelle Silver.

ISBN 978-0-545-21494-0

12 11 10 9 8 7 6 5 4 3 2 1   10 11 12 13 14 15/0

Copyright © 2010 by Girls' Life

Published by Scholastic Inc.
SCHOLASTIC and associated logos are trademarks and/or registered trademarks of Scholastic Inc.

Illustrated by Bill Thomas
Designed by Angela Jun and Molly D'Isernia
Printed in the U.S.A. 40
First printing, November 2010

contents

Introduction

You know those Magic 8-Balls? You ask a burning question, shake one up, and it gives you an answer. Should you go out with that guy from camp who just asked ya to the movies? *Most definitely.* Should you wear that ruffled minidress with those snakeskin cowboy boots to your school dance? *Outlook not so good.* It would be awesome if we had 8-Balls to make our decisions for us. After all, we make thousands of 'em a day. Gazillions over a lifetime. And whether it's a no-brainer (chips or fries with that?) or a potential life-changer (living with Mom or Dad after the divorce?), **every decision matters**—especially when you make the right ones. But **how do you reach** the point where you can safely say what you want without melting into a confused little puddle? **Here's a little science lesson:** Your brain is still developing and your thinking skills are flourishing. When used, those cerebral connections strengthen. Yep, making **consistently ace decisions** is an acquired skill. Each time you wisely choose to, say, study bio instead of mindlessly texting your BFF, you're that much closer to setting your internal dials to smart-choice automatic pilot. **Of course,** no one makes the best choice every time. But *Girls' Life* is here to steer you in the right direction and give ya all the info you need to amp up your fab decision-making skills. That way, you can handle everything from friend feuds to school sitches in a snap. So, will this book help you **take charge of every choice** and make you an even more amazing you? *All signs point to yes.*

It would be **hard to imagine** going through life without my friend Liesl. But three years ago, it was hard to imagine us in the same room. Why? Well, it all started like this:

I had met her friend Michael at a party and thought he was completely cute. A couple of phone calls and movies later, Michael and I were casually dating. One weekend, he suggested I meet him and a couple of his friends at his house. Sounded cool to me. I arrived and he was already in the kitchen with Liesl and her BFF Lisa. No problem. I introduced myself and looked forward to BBQ-ing and chilling out on his deck. *That didn't last long.*

Within ten minutes, Lisa made it clear she and Michael were tight and that the chances of me reaching that status were about nil. In between telling me about **all the crazy-fun times** she and Michael shared, Lisa sweetly hinted that I was one in a long line of girls to grace one of his grillouts. And she managed to do all this while spoon-feeding Michael potato salad. Gag.

As much as I would like to say Liesl tossed me an olive branch, she pretty much sat silently at Lisa's side. By the end of the night, I was ready to order them both a couple of cyanide lattes.

To her credit, **Lisa was right** about one thing—Michael and I lasted slightly longer than my ice cream sandwich. A couple weeks after Michael put a new girl into the BBQ rotation, I saw Liesl at the Midsummer's Night dance, standing alone in line for the bathroom.

My first thought was to run the other direction and hold it for the next five hours. But practicality and nature won out. I would love to say that I socked her with a dazzlingly witty and catty remark that left her withering. **But instead,** I said something that surprised us both: "So now that I'm no longer dating Michael, does that mean I am off your list of *persona non grata*?"

Liesl cracked up, **"Yeah, I guess it does mean that."** And with that, our friendship began anew.

Sometimes, I wonder what would have happened if I had turned back around like every fiber of my being was telling me to do—if Liesl and I would have ever become friends. I would like to think I wouldn't have let such an awesome person pass me by. But I'm pretty sure I would have ended up lumping her into the same category as her evil BFF and blown them both off. It would have been the easy thing to do.

♡KB

Making Peace with Your Parents

1

Hopefully, you have a pretty good relationship with your 'rents. But even perfect parents can be a pain once in a while. Whether they're on your case about school, pressuring ya to perform better on the field, or prying into your personal business, the whole hovering-like-a-helicopter act can get old quick.

Or maybe they're not in-your-face folks, but you're still having a **tough time** telling them what's on your mind.

Whatever the issue is, please know that in the end, *they really want what's best for you.* They just have a funny way of showing it.

So to **keep things cool** in your casa, we're here to guide you through all sorts of parental probs—and help you emerge an even more amazing daughter as a result.

Opening Up

Need the folks to back off a bit? **Here's a hint:** Screaming "Just leave me alone!", then sprinting to your room and slamming the door isn't going to work. You need a much more mature move. Here's what to do to get a grip on the sitch and *bring peace*—and quiet—between you and your 'rents.

❀ They're on your case 24/7

When your mom is *freaking for the umpteenth time* about the dirty-clothes pile in your room, it's totally tempting to tune her out. Here's our shocking advice: Do the opposite by listening to her gripe.

Truth is, you'll never nip the nagging if you don't understand where it's coming from and why. Yes, it may seem stupid that a *pile of jeans* on your floor is enough to send your mom into freakout mode, but she's trying to teach you that ya gotta take care of business. So when Mom sees you slacking, her aim is to get you back on track.

Parents often see small, irresponsible stuff as symptoms of a bigger prob. Sure, the messy state of your crib is on her mind. *More important,* though, she's worried it's a sign you'll be disorganized in other areas of life, like when it comes to handling crucial school deadlines.

So the *key* is to reassure your mom. You could say, "Mom, I know I've let my room go, but it's not because I'm flaky or lazy. I've been caught up with schoolwork, that's all. I'll clean it up this weekend." *Then, keep your promise.*

❀ They expect too much

As soon as you walk through the door from a long day at school, *Mom's asking you* to set the table and Dad wants to talk pitching strategies for your next softball game.

To get them to back off a bit, reason with your 'rents. Tell them you need some *chill time* after school before you can discuss your day or start your chores, then suggest chatting about classes after dinner or—if you're an early bird—on your way to school.

✿ They're overprotective

Your BFF is throwing her annual birthday party—and, for the *first time,* boys are invited. Your 'rents said you could go, but your mom's already let you know she'll be calling to "check in" during the party. Doesn't she have any confidence in you?

Well, sure. **Believe it or not,** your mom wants you to have a blast at the bash. Like all mothers, though, she sees you as **her little girl growing up,** and it's making her a teensy bit nervous.

The **best way** to curb her hassling you with constant calls? Reassure her all the way. Call her at convenient moments with party updates. Your mom will not only *feel relieved,* but she'll likely ease up on the hounding since she'll see you as totally trustworthy.

Reasoning with the 'RENTS

Parents putting tons of pressure on ya? Here's how to get them to listen—and maybe even back off a bit.

Pick the right time and place. Don't bring up a tense topic when anxiety levels are high in your house. Mom had a bad day at work? Wait until she's in a better place before you lay anything on her. Scheduling a chat in advance—say, over coffee or an after-dinner walk—will ensure Mom and Dad will be focused on *you*, not the five million other things on their minds.

Java Joe

Get yer Fix!

Show some respect. Your 'rents will be much more responsive if you come to them asking for advice, not accusing them of something. So instead of starting with, "You guys are just so hard on me," try simply saying, "I'm having a tough time dealing at school and hope we can talk about it." That'll show you respect their opinion, and make for a better-balanced discussion.

Stick to the subject. Pinpoint the one area that's really troubling you (like how you just can't fit in two hours of piano practice on top of school and sports) and offer details that support your side. Your parents will be more helpful if they really understand where you're coming from—and why you're so stressed.

Remain calm. If the tone turns tense, don't run to your room or fire off angry words. Listen to what Mom and Dad are saying, then offer a reasonable response, like "I understand what you're saying, but that's not how I see it."

Offer a solution. Present your parents with acceptable resolutions. Hate how they bombard you with school questions night after night? Request a weekly check-in, where you'll go through your class status, subject-by-subject. Think about an approach that'll make your life easier, while keeping them informed and in-the-loop.

Keep up the chitchat. The more you let your parents in on your world, the easier it'll be to express your worries and concerns. So try to share the ups and the downs of every day with them over dinner, or before you head to bed. That way, you'll prevent coming to blows when the really big stuff comes up.

Have It Your Way

Parents are *good at saying "no."* Can your BFF stay over? Not tonight. Will they buy you a new car when you turn sixteen? No way. Can you go away with your BF and his family for the weekend? Not a chance! So, why do they shoot you down so often? And, more crucially, how can you get a "yes" instead? Here's how to increase your chance of getting what you want. . . .

❀ Think like your parents

Try to come up with any objections they might have, and make a list. You might think **the reasons** are dumb, but jot them down anyway. Next, come up with a reasonable rebuttal for each possible objection. Also, be willing to **explain why** this is important to you.

Let's say you really want to go on spring break vacay with your BFF Kate. Don't say "everyone else" is going away. Maybe they are. **Doesn't matter**—don't say it. Try, "Kate and I never get to hang out now that she's in gymnastics three nights a week and I have orchestra practice. It's important to me that I get this chance to spend time with her." Coming up with a reason adults can relate to will boost your odds of success.

❀ Say it with savvy

Choose the right time to ask for permission. Don't ask them when they're in a hurry. Don't ask when they walk in the door after work. Don't ask in the car on the way to school. Let your parents know you want to **talk about something,** and agree on a quiet, unrushed time to chat.

Be sure not to **whine or beg.** If you speak politely, the conversation will go much better. Being respectful also means no eye-rolling, heavy sighing, or sneering. Yep, you're *eager for an answer.* But your parents might need time to think about your request. If you push them to decide immediately, the answer could very well be "no"—so don't pressure.

❀ Change their minds

After thinking it over, have the 'rents turned down your request? **First off,** don't have a hissy fit. Calmly, ask them to explain their reasoning. **Don't spark an argument** by squealing, "Why not?!" Instead say, "Can you tell me what influenced your decision?" Then, listen to their concerns. They might be bugging about a history project you have due after spring break. They could be worried about your safety. Maybe the trip interferes with family plans.

Then, for each concern, **come up with a solution.** Agree to finish your project before you go. Offer to have your friend's folks speak with yours about rules and safety. If they're adamantly opposed to your spending vacation time away from them, **compromise.** Maybe your parents will let you go on the trip for just a few days.

🌸 Put a plug in it

They've flat-out refused? That's tough—but let it go if you want any luck getting your way next time around. But if they said yes, **don't get too comfy.** You need to keep plugging away at it by keeping your word. Finish that history project. Stick to the rules that they and your friend's folks agreed on. Also, be sure to **show your gratitude.** Be specific. Tell your folks, "Thank you for trusting me." "Thank you for driving me to the airport." **Parents really do** want to do things for kids, but they like to know kids appreciate it.

Thank You

'Fessin' Up to the Folks

Getting your 'rents to *reason* with you is one thing. But getting them to forgive you for a major faux pas—and to let you out of the house before your eighteenth birthday—is another. Coming clean about **doing something wrong,** whether it's lying, cheating, stealing, or all of the above, can be as tricky as it is tough. So if you've let your folks down in a major way, here are five post-disaster strategies that can help you **resolve the stickiest of situations.**

1. Get straight to the point.

Ever have a friend rush up to you after class to tell you how crushed she is over getting a *C in history*? But before she actually gets to the C part, she has to **explain** how the teacher hates her, how the test wasn't fair, how her head was throbbing, and *blah, blah, blah?!!* The **point** is that she got a bad grade. Period. When too many details tie up the story, the truth gets confused in all the minutiae.

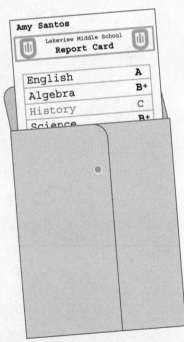

Amy Santos

Lakeview Middle School
Report Card

English	A
Algebra	B+
History	C
Science	B+

So when it comes to stuff that's going to *raise eyebrows* of disapproval, there's only one plan: Spit it out! Otherwise, parents will get lost (and probably ticked) in the buildup. *Start with these words:* "Mom and Dad, I have something important to tell you." Then tell them exactly what happened. No excuses.

2. Don't blame others.

Now that you've gotten straight to the point and confessed, *it's time for* the parents' verdict, or **"The Talk."** But don't fret. The key to getting through The Talk is to actually listen to what your parents have to say and answer third-degree questions directly.

Now is when they'll want those details (the parts we told you to tuck away for after you got the real goods out in the open) so they can get to the **bottom of the situation.**

The truth is, responsibility is what keeps the steam from shooting out of an angry parent's ears. If you don't blame the other kids who were involved and *own up to your own actions* by saying sorry, you show Mom and Dad that you didn't mean to do wrong. It's a gesture that may also, by the way, lessen punishment time and change chore lists from heavy-duty overhauling to light dusting. *Think about it.*

3. Promise it won't happen again.

When *we make mistakes,* we're supposed to learn something. Pick up a hot pan, and you betcha you'll never pick up hot stuff again *without an oven mitt!* Not rocket science.

But sometimes, lessons are more abstract and heavy, and involve emotions and other people—and it all *just gets complicated.* That's why certain promises have to be made. A promise that you won't make the same mistakes twice puts a big Band-Aid on the situation and helps rebuild trust.

That *sincere promise* is what your parents are looking for. They know you didn't mean to get tangled in trouble—it just happens sometimes. But, they also need to be reassured your latest mishap isn't a new habit that's forming. Give your 'rents your word, and mean it.

4. Wait it out.

Parents keeping you on a short leash? Still seeing the disappointment in their eyes? *After a screw-up,* it might seem like life will never get back to normal. It may take time to prove yourself again and reinstate other people's trust in you.

The key is to give your parents some time and space. Let the storm blow over. Those who care about you will almost always be willing to give you *a second chance*—but forgiveness doesn't always happen overnight. People need time to get over their anger and disappointment. Patience!

5. Live and learn.

What's the point in working your way out of a pickle if you don't learn from your mistakes? There's always a lesson in there somewhere, so take note—*no lying* to the 'rents about where you're going, no more hanging out with kids they told you not to. And when you mess up again (oh, and you will—after all, you're only human), remind yourself that at least now you know how to **accept the consequences** like a sport.

19

Sibling Rivalry

Got **brothers or sisters?** Then you've probably heard the phrase, "Why can't you be more like (insert superstar sibling's name here)" slip out of your parents' mouths.

And whether you've got a perfectionist prom queen for an older sis or an adorable (but bratty!) li'l bro, it can be challenging to **compete for time** and attention from your folks. Even if your 'rents are pretty good about spreading the love among the entire fam, when you've got siblings, you've probably got rivalry.

So if you're feeling lost in the *shadows of your sibs,* here's how to talk to your parents—and get 'em to shine the spotlight on you, too.

Uniquely YOU

One of the *most important things* you can realize is that your parents don't love you any less than your brother. Sometimes 'rents can get wrapped up comparing others—they assume if one of you is like that, why isn't the other?

Remind your parents that *it isn't a competition* between you and your brother or sister, and that you're not two of a kind.

They probably don't even realize they're making ya feel bad, so a little wake-up call can't hurt. A problem can't be corrected if they don't realize it's there.

Sharing is caring

The most important thing you can do is *share your unique accomplishments* with your fam. Got an awesome grade on a paper? Show your parents! Took some perfect pics? Post 'em on the refrigerator for all to see! This will help your 'rents realize what makes you *you*.

Speak up

Feeling like they're *treating you unfairly?* Let your parents know how it makes you feel when they give you a hard time for something—and give your sibs a seemingly easier time for the same offense. Getting blamed is no fun . . . especially if you didn't do anything wrong in the first place.

And if it's just that you want some extra time with your 'rents, speak up and *ask for it.* Schedule a standing Saturday morning bagel run with Dad, or ask Mom if she wants to take a knitting class with you. Use that together time to talk about stuff that's important to you—

you'll feel way closer to both parents, and won't be so bugged when each of your siblings get their special snaps from them. And know this: All kids feel left out sometimes (even your bro and sis), but your time to shine will come around.

Get someone on your side

If you talked to your parents and they still aren't treating you fairly, talk to a close aunt or grandparent and tell them what's going on. Maybe they have some advice to give, or maybe they will talk to your parents and let them know how upset their actions are making you. It's always good to have one relative or close friend you know you can talk to. It's also great to have an outlet for getting out your frustrations.

The Bottom Line . . .

As with any relationship, communication is key to keeping things from getting too rocky between you and your 'rents. So little by little, keep the convos flowing with the folks. Don't be afraid to share your feelings and to ask them for help when you need it. When you're confident enough to talk things over with your parents, they'll respect what a cool and together daughter they have. So keep the communication open, and not only will they let up on the nagging, but you might actually enjoy their company. Seriously.

Mom-o-Meter

OK, so your mom isn't perfect—but she's yours, and you've gotta deal with her. Take our quiz to see where your mom-relationship ranks on our scale.

1. Your mom asks her standard after-school question: "How was school today—anything exciting happen?" You . . .

A. tell her about the kid who fell asleep in math class and left a puddle of drool on his desk.

B. mumble, "Nah, just a normal day."

C. groan, "Why do you always ask me that?"

2. You're catching up on the latest IM gossip when your mom asks you to empty the dishwasher—now. You . . .

A. sign off and get right to it. She works hard and needs you to pitch in a little.

B. type a quick "Gotta go" to your chat buddies and nicely ask your mom for a fifteen-minute warning next time.

C. mutter, "I'm not your cleaning lady," and ignore her. You figure you've got a good ten minutes til she starts yelling.

3. Your guy bud (and secret crush) is throwing a party, and your mom wants to come in and say hi. You . . .

A. are stoked—now you can get your mom's take on your crush.

B. are a tad embarrassed but deal with it—you know she just wants to make sure his folks are chaperoning.

C. are utterly mortified. You insist she drop you off at the corner so no one sees the two of you together.

4. Your mom says she finds it disrespectful when you roll your eyes at her. You . . .

A. vow to drop the habit.

B. tell her you'll stop if she'll quit patting you on the head in public.

C. sigh and roll your eyes.

5. Shopping with your mom is like . . .

A. shopping with your friends—only better, 'cause Mom pays!

B. brushing your teeth. Not the most fun-filled activity, but it has to be done.

C. shoving knitting needles under your fingernails. Talk about torture!

Now tally up your answers!

Mostly A's

Smooth Sailing

You and your mom get along great! It's like having a live-in best friend. Fun! A bond of trust is crucial to any solid relationship. You value your mom enough to share secrets and tell her what's going on in your life. She trusts you, too, which means she's willing to give you some freedom. Just remember that, as cool as your mom is, close relationships with friends are important, too. If you find yourself hanging out more with Mom than with friends, it could be time to spread your social-circle wings.

Mostly B's

Middle of the Road

Seems like you and your mom have a normal, balanced relationship. You know you can count on her when the going gets tough, but you know her role is to be a parent—not necessarily a best bud. Make some extra effort to let your mom know just how much you appreciate all the stuff she does for you. Since you tell her when her nagging drives you nuts, why not say "thanks" for the ride to dance class? Stick a note in her purse, or buy her one of her fave dark chocolate bars on the way home from school. Schedule some "girl time" for just the two of you. Little things like that make moms melt and give you guys a chance to get closer.

Mostly C's

Rocky Ride

You two get along like oil and water. Mother-daughter arguments are normal at this stage, but it's definitely worth putting some effort into improving the relationship. Your mom can be your best ally at times. Of course, all fights are two-sided, but you can do your part to make peace. Next time you're tempted to blow up at your mom, remember that temper tantrums are tacky. Instead, approach her with a mature, easygoing attitude and genuinely listen to what she has to say. Believe it or not, your mom went through a lot of the same stuff you're dealing with, like mood swings and crushes and stress. Give her a chance, and open up to her—she might surprise you with her helpful advice.

Getting Guys

2

In a perfect world, the guy of your dreams will seek you out, make eye contact, and fall madly, truly, and deeply in love with you. Or at least in *like*. But hardly anything happens so easily—and sometimes it takes work to get a guy to, uh, know you exist before you can start dreaming about that first date.

So how do you score some hang time with that boy who's on your mind? And figure out if he's really right for you? All it takes is a little know-how and savvy from girls who've been through it before to get ya to that guy.

So listen up: We're taking you through from start to finish so when the time comes to approach that cutie, you'll be 100-percent ready-set-go.

Does He Like You?

You have your eye on a guy, and romance on the brain. Should you act on it? Sadly, no magical device exists to reveal whether or not a guy likes you. But if you pay attention to how he acts and follow your intuition, you'll find he's not so tough to read after all.

He's acting . . . different

You've known him forever. But, lately, he acts kinda weird. He doesn't meet your eyes when you're saying your hellos, and he can't shut up about the weather. Or he's the opposite—completely clammed up. This shift could be a sign that his feelings toward you have changed . . . from *amigo* to *amour*.

On the know

It's the day of your giant English presentation on *Macbeth*. As you sit in history sneakily reviewing your notes, your crush whispers, "Good luck today!" Thing is, he's not even in your English class. If he's all of a sudden in-the-know about you and your whereabouts, that means he's paying attention.

Hello there

You're at lunch when you catch a flash of pearly whites from across the hall. **He's smiling at you!** Then, he moves to sit next to you at the assembly. He's going out of his way to make contact? It could mean he's digging on you.

The grapevine

Your BFF Samantha just talked to your crush's pal Jordan, and word on the street is that **the object of your affection thinks you're pretty awesome** (yay!). It may not be the most reliable way to get info, but a little hearsay counts for somethin'.

Blushworthy crush stories!

"**During lunch,** I was staring at my crush. He turned around, saw me, and smiled. I blushed and turned away quickly, but my friend was right there and we bonked heads."

• • • • • • • •

"**I was sitting** on a railing outside school waiting for my ride. My crush walked up behind me and grabbed my shirt. It startled me and I fell off the railing. I didn't have time to put my hand in front of me, so I went face-first onto the pavement."

• • • • • • • •

"**An adult I was** sitting next to told a funny joke and I cracked up—and spit all over my crush who was sitting on the other side of me."

29

Making Your Move

So now that you've got your fella figured out (well, kinda), it's time to score some hang time with him. We've devised a plan to do just that, based on three **common crush categories**. The boy you can't get off your brain probably fits nicely into one.

The Mystery Man

The man of mystery is the boy you sorta know who smiles at you . . . once in a while. So you smile back. Sometimes (wow!) he even waves. Does he like you but is afraid to tell you? Or is he friendly to a lot of girls? How can you crack this case and find out if he's for you?

◆ *Low-risk move:* Just before your next school dance, when he says "Hi" or smiles, stop him. Ask if he's going to the dance. Even if he says, "I dunno, maybe," you can respond with a confident, "OK, well, maybe I'll see you there." Then smile, say, "Later!" and walk away.

◈ **Medium-risk move:** Repeat the low risk move, but when he answers, say, "I was hoping you were going . . . so I could maybe dance with you." Even if he'd rather eat glass than go to the dance, now he knows you want more than a wave between third and fourth periods.

◈ **High-risk move:** Ask him to the dance . . . as your date. He's going with his buds? Tell him to save you a dance. Then, approach him on the big night and boldly ask him to bust a move.

The Friend

This is the guy who's around a lot—with your group of friends, on your block, in homeroom, wherever. You're probably already buds, but lately you've been thinking it'd be fun to graduate him to boyfriend material. But how?

◆ *Low-risk move:* He's no stranger—you guys talk a bunch. So paying him just a bit more attention shouldn't scare him away or trip you up. Ask him about the stuff you know he's into ("How long have you been playing the drums?"). Do it on a good hair day, and look at his lips a lot when he's talking. And smile!

◆ *Medium-risk move:* Since you two are friendly, talk to him about a subject only friends share: crushes. Ask how old he was when he had his first crush. Who was it? Make the conversation playful, so he's not uncomfortable. Good. Now you have him thinking about that and you at the same time.

◆ *High-risk move:* Ask him out. With a buddy, you can say it in a not-so-serious way: "I wanted to invite you for pizza, but I thought that might be extra cheesy. Wanna do sushi instead?" You might catch him off guard, so tell him he can get back to you on it. Then hope.

The Good Guy

You sort of know him, but he's not officially a friend. He's the boy who rides your bus, your science lab partner, the youth club cutie. You're around him enough to know you like what you see. And you're pretty sure he's into you, too.

⊕ **Low-risk move:** Do nothing. Look, a crush is a crush because there's no risk in putting your heart out there. You can keep seeing him where you see him and dig on the thrill of having a cute boy to crush on. It's fun and fine the way it is.

⊕ **Medium-risk move:** Think of something bona fide to borrow. Make up the excuse that you're cold—and ask if he can lend you his hoodie. Then, return it to him with a nice thank you note.

⊕ **High-risk move:** Figure out a way to be alone with him so he can get to know you as you, not as the girl who sits next to him in biology. Ask him if he wants to study together for the upcoming test: "Dude, I need your smarts to help me come up with a good system for remembering this junk." Flattery will get you . . . alone with him in the library.

Get Flirty!

Quick tips to get your guy's attention

Catch his gaze and flash a smile when you see him. Check out his reaction: Does he hold your gaze and smile back? If so, good. Repeat this process a couple times, until one of you is bold enough to strike up a conversation.

Branch out. Guys are put off by groups of loud girls, so break away and give him a chance to approach you on your own.

Ask intelligent questions. The key is to act interested and be interesting. If you're stuck on what to say, think of questions you like to be asked and ask those.

Say his name. If you want to bond with your flirt partner, say his name during the conversation. It's a subtle signal that you want to connect.

Lighten up. Humor is the best tool for flirting, and you don't have to be a comedian to use it in an effective way. Simply show him your lighter, funnier side with easy—not forced—smiles and laughs.

Dating Dos and Don'ts

So the moves worked and—yeah!—you've scored a date! But wait, what on earth are you gonna do on date night? First, get a grip. He wouldn't have asked you out if he didn't have a clue that **you're a great girl.** So show him just how divine you really are, darling!

Easy Does It

It's great you have so many things you want to do on the date—ice skating, eating at that new Mexican restaurant, checking out an awesome local band—just don't plan them all for the same date. Instead, pick one or two and concentrate on having a great time. Save the rest for a second date —and hopefully a third and a fourth. . . .

✱ Shake it up

If you guys don't know each other well already, plan an activity. Going to an arcade or bowling is a whole lot less stressful than staring each other down over dinner. After your tenpin tourney, suggest going for coffee. That way, you get some face time following all the fun 'n' games.

✱ All together now

It can be way intimidating to hang out with a guy one-on-one. So if it puts you at ease, make it a group thing and you each can invite friends along. Just don't abandon your date in favor of the comfort of BFFs. Sit next to him at the movie and pizza place. You *are* on a date!

Clothes Call

Don't bust your bank on an all-new ensemble. What to wear is all about picking the perfect outfit—for you. (*Psst* . . . want to know more about lookin' fierce? Check out our style and beauty tips in Chapter Five!)

✳ Make the right choice

Going to a concert? Sure, your high heels are rock-star hot, but leave 'em home—hello, you'll be standing. Are you two catching up on TiVo and ordering a pizza? A miniskirt isn't the best choice for lounging on the couch.

✳ Comfort is key

Your skinny black pants and off-the-shoulder shirt shave off, like, ten pounds. Problem is, you can't sit down very well in the pants and the shirt doesn't stay put. So leave 'em in the closet. Instead, pick one unique piece with your normal cute wear, like dark jeans with a fancy beaded top. You'll look extra-special but feel like yourself.

✳ Ask for help

If you're really baffled about what to wear, call the girls over for a dress rehearsal. Pick someone you trust to tell it like it is ("That green is not your best color."). If you can't find a thing to wear in your closet, borrow something.

Say, Huh?

Worried the two of you will have nothing to talk about? Yeah, awkward. But don't worry—you can keep the convo going. . . .

Don't be a copycat

Nothing wrong with being polite when he talks about his passion for football. Just don't act like you're into it, too, if you don't know the difference between a touchdown and a first down. You're going to have different interests, and that's part of what makes dating fun. But if you fake it too much, sooner or later he'll catch on that you're pretending to be someone you're not. And no one wants to date a phony.

Ask away

Does he play a musical instrument? Have any brothers or sisters? Want to be an astronaut? People like to talk about themselves, so you can't go wrong by asking him questions. Then, listen.

So . . . um . . . yeah . . .

Beforehand, think of a few things to chat about when those inevitable silences happen. Maybe talk about the killer bio exam or a new band you're into. When spending time with someone in a new way, it can be uncomfortable at first. If you come prepared with mental notes, you'll have something to say. No need to be a chatterbox—just have convo starters in case you need 'em.

Gabbing with guys . . . gauge your style

No doubt, there's pressure when it comes to talking to guys. So . . . how well do *you* handle it?

1. A guy you've had your eye on is headed your way with a smile. You . . .
A) calmly say, "Hey," and then start up a convo.
B) whisper, "What a hottie," to your friend.
C) flash a smile, and then panic.
D) don't even notice him—you're late for practice.

2. You're chatting with your crush, and there's a lull in the conversation. You . . .
A) fire off a question. You've mentally filed some away for just this moment.
B) point out a teacher in the hall to poke fun at, just to say something.
C) cross your fingers and hope he'll save the convo.
D) say, "See ya!"

3. You've never talked to your crush on the phone, but his number is flashing on the caller ID. You . . .
A) grab it after the second ring. The moment you've been waiting for is here!

B) answer it, trying to keep the giggles under control.

C) debate whether you should pick it up, because you're suddenly having a panic attack.

D) pick up. You need to ask him something about the chem homework.

4. You're on the phone with your BFF when she notices your crush has just logged on. You . . .

A) thank your BFF, and then get online to say, "Hey."

B) jump online and IM him. You're tons more comfy chatting with him this way.

C) sign on, just in case he decides to send you a message.

D) figure you'll catch him next time you're online.

5. You're dying to know if your crush is going to the Valentine's dance with someone. You . . .

A) mention the dance to see if he spills the beans.

B) convince your friend to ask him for you.

C) worry about it until you see him at the dance.

D) just ask him if he's going.

Answers

Mostly A's • Gettin' to know you
As a chitchatty kinda gal, your open, friendly attitude is great for smooth encounters with your crush. Talking to your crush probably comes just as easily as talking to your BFF. So what's your next step? Catch him in the hall or at his locker for chats, or invite him to hang out at the mall with you and your friends. Just remember, there's no need to rush a crush by coming on too strong.

Mostly B's • Gettin' the giggles
You're not always shy, just guy-shy. Build up your conversation confidence by getting to know guys as friends first—even the ones you have crushes on. If there is one particular guy who sends you into bubble zone, try your best to remember that he's just a regular person who wants to know the real you—not the giggle gal.

Mostly C's • Gettin' goose bumps
Ever dash into the girls' bathroom to avoid running into your favorite cutie? Thought so. It's natural to panic when confronted by your crush, but you're also cutting off chances to make a real connection. Pause and think about what you're going to say before blurting out the first thing that pops into your head. And try to approach him in group situations to alleviate the fear factor.

Mostly D's • Gettin' to the point
Your no-nonsense, direct approach could be a big boost with your crush—you'll spend much less time dropping hints or hiding your feelings. The next time you're tempted to cut a conversation short, ask him what he thought of the school play or last night's big game. It will show him you're into what he has to say, and it might give him some extra time to work up the nerve to ask what you're up to this weekend.

Sealed With A Kiss

Let's say the date is a dream, and there you are at the doorway with your dude just staring into each other's eyes. Is it time for that perfect goodnight kiss? Well, it depends. The decision when, where, and how to smooch is totally up to you. So listen to your instincts, trust your gut, and make the choice that you're completely comfy with. You'll know when the time is right.

When He Doesn't Return the Feelings

You talked, you laughed, there might have even been a goodnight kiss. But now he's telling you that it's not going to work out, and you feel slammed. Everyone's advice to "not worry about it" isn't helping. Before you swear off guys completely, get real: You're gonna go on some bad dates, get rejected (probably more than once), and go through some tough breakups. But don't freak out too much, because there will be good times, too. Promise.

OK, the first thing you have to do is fully face the fact that your crush is not into having you as a girlfriend. Period. You don't want to wallow in denial, so let go of any wishful fairytale thinking. Don't dwell on mythological "maybe he'll like me next week" thoughts. And don't try to change yourself so he'll notice you. You are who you are, and it's his loss he's not into it.

Banish him from your brain

Fill your mind with happy thoughts that don't include him. From this point on, he is your ex-crush. Visions of him are off-limits in your daydreams, his name is never again to be penciled in your notebook, and his school picture must promptly be removed from the inside of your locker. No more endless discussions with your buds—his name is now banished from your convos. And, while you have little control over random run-ins at school, you must stop strategically planting yourself in the bleachers during his soccer practice.

Ease up on the sappy stuff

Who doesn't love a romantic movie? But at this stage of the game, that tearjerker isn't going to help your cause any. It will only bring on thoughts of your crush just when you are doing the mind-erase thing. Next time you're in the video store, head for the comedy section. That saying about laughter being the best medicine is hokey but true, especially for shaking the blues. And when tuning in the stereo, stay away from sentimental stations. The last thing you need to hear is weepy music about shattered hearts.

Three Guys to Turn Down

Sure, he's cute, but he's also got a history of breaking hearts. So don't go there, girl!

The Player. This guy's super-smooth, making him popular with the ladies. Too popular. Date him and you'll just wind up another member of his ever-evolving fan club.

The Cheater. He may have kiss-and-dissed his last girlfriend, but this time's different, right? Well, not always. Unfortunately, it's pretty likely that a guy who's cheated before will become a repeat offender.

The Super-Flirt. Yeah, he may just be uber-sweet and outgoing, but be warned: He may also be giving that Prince Charming act to many other admirers.

✦ Keep busy

Take up knitting, study Swahili, invest in some jogging shoes. This is a perfect time to kick off a new activity. It'll keep you focused on something other than those feelings of rejection. A really good bet? Dedicate time to people who are in need. Offer to help Grandma get her tomatoes planted, or make your famous tuna casserole for a neighbor who's been sick. Giving to others will make you feel all warm inside and definitely beats the boy-blues.

✦ Turn to friends and fam

A fantasy romance is no substitute for people who truly love and care for you in real life. Finding out a crush doesn't dig you can do a number on your self-esteem. So spending time with people who adore you is a reminder that, hey, you rock! Plan a sleepover with your pals, or challenge your brother to a video game. (Beating your bro three times in a row should make you feel great!)

The Bottom Line . . .

Face it, the dating game is tricky with all those twists and turns. But the thing is, as stressful as it can be, it should be fun, too. So be easy on yourself when things don't go as planned—and no matter what, never change who you are for a guy. It sounds cliché, but being cool with yourself is the most attractive quality a girl can have. Be genuine, be relaxed, and don't be afraid to show him that you've got a sense of humor. Let him see the true-blue essence of you! Being comfortable and confident with who you are sends out the best message of all.

Making Your Friendships Fab

3

You can't imagine a world without your girls. You're BFFs and, as far as you're concerned, you guys rule *Friendship Paradise.*

But your friendship can weather some **tropical storms,** too. Maybe you've been bickering over the dumbest things. Or perhaps you don't get as much hang time since you go to separate schools now. Stressful stuff you can't control can be tough on a friendship.

But what if **something came up** that could affect your friendship and you could control it? Would you make the right choice?

Would you **spill** if you saw her boyfriend holding hands with another girl? Would you let the teacher know you saw her cheating during finals? What's a girl to do when faced with a **major BFF dilemma?**

We've dug around to find the **stickiest sitches** you may deal with when it comes to your buds—and how to make wise choices about each and every one of 'em.

Under Pressure

Peer pressure. It's hard to escape sometimes. Even harder when it's your very best pal piling it on. While your BFF's been a *fabulous influence* in the past (like when she talked you into going out for track—and guess who made varsity?), her idea of fun is *starting to be a stretch.* That doesn't mean you have to give in to her—or give up on your friendship. Here's a guide to standing strong when your BFF tries to break ya out of your comfort zone.

BFF

Pressure Point: *Social studies is a total snoozefest—at least according to your bud. She's cutting and wants you to join.*

Sitting in class may be a big bore, but so is detention. The next time your girl grabs ya and heads for the door, remind her that her parents are probably going to freak out if she gets caught. Plus, she likely needs a partner in crime, so *showing you won't give in will make her back down.* And if not? Well, she'll learn.

Pressure Point: **Your pal's constantly snooping for homework answers—and you're her number one go-to.**

Newsflash! Cheaters only cheat themselves. Instead of giving your smarts away, *offer to be study buddies* with your girl. This way, if she has legit questions (not just, "What's the answer to number four?"), you'll be there to help. You can never fail for trying, and believing in her may be the ego boost she needs to start making studying more her scene.

Pressure Point:

Your girl is a super-shopper, compelling you to drop dollars even though your parents are strict about spending.

While it's great to ogle over trendy threads and hot new gadgets, it's best (for you and your wallet) to *shop smart.* So when ya hit the mall together, take a gander at the pricier items, then *hit the sale racks.* And if she pressures ya to make a big purchase? Offer up a simple excuse like, "I'll get those jeans after my next baby-sitting gig," and move along.

Pressure Point: She's tons of fun to hang out with, but when the clock strikes 10 P.M. and your curfew's calling, she begs you not to go.

Sure, curfews might be lame, but not as much as tampering with your parents' respect. And while your girl might not have to follow similar rules, you need to keep consequences in check. Made curfew five times in a row? Try asking Mom for an hour extension next time.  Or request a flexible check-in time one Saturday a month in exchange for extra chores or great grades. Showing that you're reliable will keep your parents' trust, making them more likely to be lenient. If all else fails, try making plans with your friend earlier in the evening. Remind her that what matters most is being together, not where or what time.

Pressure Point: She's been getting into bad stuff like smoking and drinking alcohol, and wants you to do it, too.

If a BFF has been getting into some shady biz, steer clear. Sometimes buds take a turn in the wrong direction and get in tonsa trouble. If your girl invites you to, say, a keg party in the woods? A simple "No, but thanks anyway" will suffice. It's worth a shot to ask if she'll embark on a movie marathon instead. She won't budge? Put the friendship on ice for now.

Confronting Your Chicas

So perhaps peer pressure isn't your pal prob. Maybe it's simply the fact that there's just something amiss among your crew and you need to make a move—fast!—or your friendship could go down like the *Titanic.*

Is your bud doing something that's really buggin' ya? Are you feeling left out? Do you have to spill something supersensitive to her and you're just not sure how to? It's never easy to approach your girl about uncomfortable issues, but in most cases, gathering that courage to chat will help save your relationship—and, likely, make it more fab than it already is. Here's how to handle some typically touchy topics.

"My BFF is so bossy! She's always telling me what to wear, who to be friends with, and which clubs to join. How can I get her to back off a bit?"

Control freak, much? Friends who take the lead and plan fun stuff are great. But she should never make decisions for ya—that's your job. So next time your girl chimes in with some unsolicited advice, *speak up!* Instead of staying mum, make some noise. She wants to see a movie, when you'd rather go shopping? Say so! You're sick of going to the theater. Every. Single. Saturday. You want to dig for discounts for a change of pace . . . so tell her.

❦

"I met a new girl a few weeks ago and she invited me to her birthday party, but none of my other friends. Should I go?" Why not? It's totally OK to *hang with girls outside your crew.* Branching out into different social circles brings out other aspects of your personality. It demonstrates, even if only to yourself, that your identity is not dependent on a certain group of people. You can mix it up, right?

❦

"I've heard nasty rumors about my friend. Should I tell her or not say anything?"

This is a delicate situation. You don't want your friend to react badly and take it out on you. On the other hand, you want to have your friend's back. If things were being tossed around school about you, **would you want to know** or would you want your friends to keep you in the dark? Answer that and you'll know what to do.

The Bud BLEND

Gain an extra bud or two this year? Here's how to blend buds the drama-free way.

Merry Merging. Ease everyone into the transition. First, check with both sides to make sure they're open to meeting. Chances are, they'll be into it. But asking before introducing shows you're taking their feelings into consideration—not just yours.

Nix Cliques. When you do bring all of your buds together, some of your old friends may stick together out of habit instead of reaching out to the new girls. To make sure no one's left out, start up casual convos on common-ground topics, like the latest celeb gossip. That way, the new girls can easily chime in without feeling clueless.

Party On. Once all the intros have been made, kick-start the new friendship by inviting everyone over for a sleepover. Giving your girls another opportunity to bond outside of school will really help seal the deal.

Reality Check. If your attempts to blend buds backfire, don't feel like you have to now pick one pal over another. It's totally cool to have a few crews of friends to hang with. After all, variety is the spice of life!

"My BFF and I both auditioned for the lead in the school play. She got it—and I'm in the chorus. I want to be happy for her, but I can't help feeling upset. I really wanted that part!"

It's *natural* to feel a twinge of jealousy when someone else gets what you really want—and you feel like you deserved it. Especially when that someone is a close friend and you have to be right there with her as she celebrates the good news. But if that green monster prevents you from being happy for her then, well, what kind of friend are you? *Your bud's successes should be a victory for you, too,* just like your big moments should be a huge deal for her.

55

"My friend shared some crazy-juicy gossip with me and I'm dying to tell someone, even though she made me promise not to say a word. It wouldn't be so bad if I mentioned it to our mutual friend, right?"

A true bud should know when to keep the lips zipped. If personal info about your friend gets out and you're the only one who knew the info, your friendship will be officially damaged—maybe beyond repair. Everyone slips now and again but when it really counts, you should be able to take the silence test and pass with flying colors. Your friend trusted you with her news because she probably figured you're a loyal and honest friend who won't go and spread it around. You'd want the same from her.

"I caught my friend cheating on a Spanish exam. Should I tell the teacher?"

Yes, cheating is wrong. But do you want your new nickname to be "Rat"? Could you deal with the fallout if she discovered you're the one who told? It's not your place to be class cop, but if you tell her that you saw her sneaking a peek at your Scantron, she'll think twice about doing it in the future. If your school has an **honor code,** your decision should be a little clearer. Most schools with honor codes take cheating very seriously. It's also serious if a teacher finds out you knew someone was cheating and kept quiet— even if it was your BFF. In such a situation, **you know the right thing to do.** We'll leave it at that.

"My BFF and I have had a crush on the same guy for, well, forever. I just heard that he likes me and is going to ask me out. Should I say yes?"

Crushin' on the same guy as your bud can be super-fun—the two of you watching for him in the halls, reporting on his every move. But if he starts returning feelings for one of you, it's a ticking time bomb. Most friendships aren't strong enough to handle the jealousy. If one of you does end up going out with him, **open communication and honesty** between you and your friend are essential. But we're here to tell ya, despite all your best efforts, it might not work. If you find yourself in this precarious place, ask yourself: Is going for it with a guy worth sacrificing your friendship? The answer will almost always be never. Even if he is amazing.

"I have two BFFs, and lately it seems like they spend so much time with each other—without inviting me. I feel so left out. Should I say something?"

Most definitely. Get to the bottom of their bad-bud behavior by saying something like, "Lately, I feel like you and Cassie are pushing me away. I really value our friendship and hope that if either of you has a problem with me, you'll let me know." Easier said than done, right? Resist the urge to e-mail or IM your concerns. You're much more likely to get a *straight and truthful answer* in person. And once you've cleared the air, you can stop wasting your time worrying —regardless of the outcome.

And if that doesn't work? Take a fearless look at your sitch and decide if your two best buds have been treating you in a way that is genuinely respectful. If they're not returning phone calls or including you in their plans to hit the mall for the clearance sales, something's up. Sad but true— *sometimes, friends grow apart.* Yes, it's painful to think these girls, who've been so important to you for so long, might not be a part of your life anymore. You must, must, must cut ties with anyone who doesn't value you as a true friend.

5 Golden Rules of FRIENDSHIP

Commit these to memory, and you'll be good to go, girl!

1. Don't steal your friend's guy. Do you want to keep your BFF, well, forever? Then steer clear of her crush/BF/ex. Nothing good will come of this. Ever.

2. Don't ditch your BFF for your BF. Yeah, it takes work to balance your boy and your buds, but the effort is well worth it, especially when you need support from your sistahs (hello, breakups!).

3. Stand up for your besties. Even if the most popular girl in school decides your BFF is lame, a true friend will still be her number-one fan. Stick right by her side, and she'll no doubt return the favor should someone decide to trash your rep one day.

4. Be there for them. If your BFF is having serious issues, do what you can to help her out, whether it's listening to her vent or talking to a school counselor about how a tough sitch can be fixed.

5. Be yourself. A friend's not a friend if she doesn't like you for you. Ditch the urge to put on an act, and let your lovely self shine through to the girls who are lucky enough to call themselves your besties.

Bad Buds

Even the best of friends screws up on occasion. She borrows your fave blazer without asking. She might blab a secret or say something to embarrass you in front of the whole crew. And while, at times, you'd like to shred her favorite sweater with a fork, you know your bud isn't flawless. *Friends mess up.*

But there is another kind of "friend"—one who causes you to question your worth, or often leaves you feeling upset or bummed. If you have a bud that sucks the fun out of almost anything or just makes you feel icky, she is what we call a *toxic friend.*

It could be something subtle—like her making fun of your hair or your clothes on a regular basis. Or maybe she stole your boyfriend, copied your science lab, or spread nasty (totally untrue!) rumors about you.

Toxic friends come in all varieties, but whatever the type, *they almost always never belong in your life.* So what to do if you've got one? Many girls feel intimidated to make the split. And while any breakup is hard, you can make it less stressful.

Step **1** ***Figure out what's wrong.*** What, specifically, bugs you about your friend? Is her behavior malicious or just annoying (there's a huge diff between spreading lies and, say, snoring at sleepovers)? Does your friend have wonderful qualities to balance the bad ones? Have you told her what is bothering you and asked her to change?

Before tossing a relationship, it's often worth trying to set things straight. And even if you ultimately decide the friendship can't be salvaged, you will have clearly thought through the situation. This will make the next step that much easier. . . .

Step **2** ***Say sayonara.*** It's time to part ways? Offer a short and simple explanation, and then state that you want to end the friendship: "I've asked you to stop saying mean things to me. It makes me feel terrible. I'm sorry, but I don't want to be friends anymore." Be clear and calm, and don't verbally attack, which could cause things to spiral out of control and leave you feeling even worse.

Step 3 *Expect the worst.* Even if you say your piece kindly and rationally, do not expect your friend to take it well. Nobody likes rejection, and your friend is no different. She'll likely defend her actions. If you think deep down she might have a valid point (maybe you did jump to a wrong conclusion or misjudge her), you might say, "Let me think about it, and let's talk again tomorrow."

You might decide your friend deserves another chance after all, and maybe this is the wakeup call she needs to turn things around. You're allowed to change your mind . . . or stick with your original plan. But in the end, you have to do what you feel is best for you.

Step 4 *Allow yourself to grieve.* If you do end the friendship, you might feel a ton of emotions after your talk. Many girls feel a mixture of relief and also guilt, sadness, or anxiety. This is normal. It shows you're a caring person who doesn't like hurting others. And even though she wasn't an ideal bud, you might even miss the good parts of her.

So allow time to mourn the loss of this relationship. Talk to a parent or other buds about it—without bad-mouthing your ex-friend. And give yourself a big pat on the back. It's not easy to get rid of toxic buds, but know that you did what's best for No. 1—you!

10 Warning Signs That You Have A Toxic Friend

1. You don't feel good about yourself when you're with her.
2. You feel drained around her, not energized.
3. You don't feel like you can totally be yourself around her.
4. The relationship feels unbalanced—the attention always has to be on her.
5. She has different values and morals than you do.
6. She's not genuinely happy when something really good happens to you.
7. She monopolizes all of your time.
8. Lying comes easily to her.
9. She blames you when things go wrong.
10. She makes you feel guilty for having other friends.

The Bottom Line . . .

Even if you have the most fabulous best friend in the whole world, sometimes your relationship is going to fall flat. There may be fights. She may get on your nerves. You may even question why you're even friends with her.

But if things aren't quite awesome between you and your bud, don't make the mistake of thinking the relationship is over. Even the best of friendships take a lot of hard work, communication, and patience. Of course, there are going to be some friends that come and go. But the truest-bluest gal pals? They really are Best Friends Forever.

Are you a true-blue bud?

Think you've got your BFF's back 24/7? Take this quiz to be sure she can depend on you in any sitch.

1. Jenna, the leader of the coolest clique in class, asks you and your new best girl, Beth, to a sleepover with her crew. Beth confides she doesn't wanna go because she's secretly afraid of the dark. When Jenna asks why Beth bagged, you say . . .

A. "She's too chicken to sleep without a nightlight!"

B. "Uh, I don't know . . . Maybe you should ask her why."

C. "She's feeling kinda sick—must be those funky tuna tacos the lunch lady dished out."

2. Your bud Meghan has been crushing on class hottie Matt. Problem is, he's never said a word to her—but he has been chatting you up big-time. Should you go there?

A. Of course! Matt is totally fair game.

B. It's probably OK, as long as you let Meghan know you and Matt like each other.

C. No way! Stealing her crush would be lower than low.

3. Grace, the most evil chick in your gym class, spreads an untrue rumor that your best pal, Lindsay, stuffs her bra. How do you help Lindsay deal?

A. You stay outta the whole thing. Grace might broadcast a big lie about you next.

B. You tell Lindsay not to sweat it—the whole thing is bound to blow over in a week or two.

C. You get right up in Grace's grill and tell her to quit.

4. You and Carly have been planning an ice-skating outing for weeks. Just as you are about to leave, your BF calls with last-minute tix to an NBA game! What the heck do you do?

A. Tell your boyfriend to pick you up right away. You want to hit the concession stand before the game starts!

B. On your way to the game, you try to call Carly to see if you can reschedule.

C. Tell your BF you can't make it. You know how psyched Carly is for skating, and you're not going to let her down.

5. Your BFF Sara is suffering a major math meltdown. Her average is in the basement. How do you help her deal?

A. You don't. You've got your own tough classes.

B. You suggest maybe her folks could spring for a tutor.

C. You head to her house every day after school and go over probs with her until she gets it.

Answers

Mostly A's
I LOVE ME
You're the kind of chick who takes care of her own biz first and foremost. Want to earn your bud's confidence for real? Put all your self-interest aside for one week, and totally be there for her. Show her she's important to you. That's called meeting you halfway—and it's what friendship is really all about.

Mostly B's
HOT 'N' COLD
Your heart's in the right place when it comes to wanting to be there for her. It's just that your actions can be a little hit-or-miss. Make a major effort to focus completely on what she's saying when she comes to you about a sitch. Think over any advice, answers, or remarks you dole out to her before they leave your lips. This is the very best way you can prove yourself to be dependable and show her how much she really matters to you.

Mostly C's
THE REAL DEAL
When it comes to comin' through, no bud does it better than you. You're there for your girl 100 percent—you're willing to put your own wants and needs aside when she really needs your time and energy. You're totally honest but know how to deliver any piece of news with kindness, smarts, and tact. Just make sure you get the same great stuff in return.

Dream Catching

Remember those dream catchers you may have had when you were little? They were made of wood and yarn and cotton, and the story goes that if you wish hard enough, your dreams will be caught in them—and come true.

While that's a lovely thought, these days **you definitely don't need a lucky charm** to make your dreams a reality. You can be and do and *go after everything you want*—as long as you know the right way to go about doing that.

In this chapter, we'll guide ya through *getting exactly what you want.* And guess what? It's not as hard as you think.

TRY OUTS THIS FRIDAY!

YOU CAN BE A STAR!

Stop Dreaming, Start Doing

You spend tons of time fantasizing about how amazing it would be to have a cool new crew, snag a supersweet BF, star in the school play . . . but then you're quickly snapped back to real life. *Sigh.*

The idea of putting in all the *effort it takes* to change up your life totally freaks you out, not to mention the fact that you don't have a clue about kicking off the steps ya gotta take to make cool stuff happen.

But here's the thing: You can curl up like a slug and do a whole lotta *nada*—or figure out how to use your dreamy aspirations as way-powerful motivation. Here's how to turn those fantasies into a reality.

Set Realistic Goals

Goals are amazing ways to set yourself up for success—but aiming too high can just make ya feel like a failure if you don't reach 'em. Rather than say, "I want to end world hunger," think, "I want to start a program to collect food for the homeless in my city." Then break your dream into smaller, attainable goals.

For example, you could create a list of grocery stores and restaurants that may be willing to donate food regularly, contact people with cars who might help you pick up the food, and find volunteers to sort the food. Before you know it, you'll have reached that dream.

Failure is Your Friend

Now that you've mapped out the road to Dreamland, your stomach is doing crazy-nervous somersaults—which is totally natural. After all, committing yourself to chasing a dream means taking a chance—you could fail big-time. Ugh. But here's a little-known secret: Failure can be a good thing.

Want proof? Grab a sheet of paper, and draw a line down the middle. On one side, list three things you always wished you'd tried, but never had the nerve. Like the time you wanted to ask your crush to the spring dance but were afraid he'd say no . . . so you had to watch him boogie the night away with that obnoxious girl from your class.

On the other side of the page, list three things you did try but didn't work out. Remember last semester when you asked to switch to honors math? Your grade sank from an A to a C.

Write down what you learned from each of your "failures." OK, maybe you weren't ready for advanced Algebra, but you definitely learned what you need to study up on so you can give it another shot next time. Now compare the two lists. Crystal clear you got so much more out of trying and failing than you did out of never taking a plunge at all? Yep.

Give Your Brain a Break

Carefully considering the moves you need to make to score big? Smart. Overthinking everything? Not so much.

Say you've thoroughly outlined the short story you're going to enter in your school's creative writing contest. You've completely developed your story's characters, have every plot point planned—yet you haven't written a single sentence. You will tomorrow, though—ooh, wait, though, you need to go over everything just one more time. . . .

Stalling much? Yup, that's what you're up to—but don't bum. Lots of girls come down with a case of the jitters right before majorly leaping from dreamin' to doin'. As soon as you start dragging even a little bit (or—yikes!—talking yourself out of the goal-getting process), clear your head and jump in.

Sit down on the spot, open your laptop, and type out that opening sentence.. Then keep on tapping away—you can always go back later to fix whatever. The point is, sometimes you have to jolt yourself out of your safety zone. The best part? You'll feel so incredibly pumped and proud once you have a completed manuscript to present.

Not So Fast—Come In Last

When you're trying to accomplish the thing you want most, you want instant results, right? Right—that's your first instinct. To truly make it, though, your best bet is to slow yourself waaaaaaay down.

When you're cruising down Big Dream Drive, you must pay attention to every sign, direction, and signal to get to your destination. If you try to rush or skip the essentials, you'll run out of gas before you get there.

So don't make time a factor. Focus instead on fully finishing whatever you're working on for the moment. No clock watching allowed! You're trying to make captain of the b-ball team? Sure, your competition, Amanda, has tons of natural talent, but you know your strength is in perfecting those moves you don't feel you've aced quite yet.

Instead of obsessing about how easily Amanda drains buckets, tell yourself, "I'm gonna spend whatever time it takes to sink twenty free throws today. Tomorrow, I'll sink thirty!" Key to reaching any dream-come-true is consistency—regularly investing time will stretch your efforts that much longer. So be patient—it'll ultimately pay off.

Now What?

Ya did it! You aced your plan to upgrade your social life, and now you're a member of the cool clique you always wanted to hang with. Thing is, now that you've gotten what you want . . . well, you're not so sure you want it. Turns out the girls you're hangin' with are totally fake. You worked so hard to make buds with everybody—what a waste.

But wait. It wasn't a time-waster. It's key to shake disappointment. So your new friends turned out to be less than stellar. Take the knowledge you've learned to be on the lookout for girls who are good friend material based on stuff other than their social status.

The coolest thing about going after a goal isn't getting what you want in the end—it's seeing what great stuff you're made of. Besides discovering what you need (or don't need)—you learn how much determination and strength you have. So go out there and use it, girl!

Get Yourself Together

Ever wish you were the girl who has it all? You know who we're talking about—the Totally Together Girl (or TTG for short). She's straight-A smart, class prez, and even volunteers at an animal shelter. You want hate her, but truth is, you kind of want to be her. Well, even if you're not totally on top of everything these days that doesn't mean you can't become just as, well, perfect as your ultra-organized classmate. Here's how to do it.

7 Secrets to Success

1. Use Your Talents. Figure out what you're good at—whether it's giving advice, creating art, or playing an instrument. Then make a real commitment to use and perfect your talents.

2. Create and Keep Deadlines. Having set deadlines will help keep you on track and give you a "finish line" to work toward.

3. Seek Advice. Don't be afraid of asking for help when you need it—whether it's from your parents, friends, or your own customers if you have a business. People will be happy to share their insight.

4. Stay Focused. Be diligent and take yourself seriously. Try to minimize distractions to get things done well and quickly. Your dream is important to you, so it demands your full attention and loyalty.

5. Be Passionate. Get others excited about your dream. Use your enthusiasm to recruit a team to help you and to gather supporters—whether it's financial supporters or cheerleaders.

6. Relax and Have Fun. While you're working toward making your dream come true, remember to take some time out. Go for a run, hang out with friends, see a movie—anything to clear your head. By staying relaxed, your mind will be refreshed and prepared to tackle anything.

7. Believe In Yourself. Because if you won't, who will? There'll always be naysayers. Stay focused on your goal, be confident, and trust yourself.

75

Here's how to do it.

TTG Secret No. 1:
She does away with distractions

You'd so study for your Spanish test, but your fave TV show is on and your pedi's in desperate need of a top coat. What's a girl to do? Well, TTG's gonna focus on the important stuff—like schoolwork, natch—first. Save the toes and shows for Saturday (that's what TiVo is for!), and tackle tasks with a definite deadline.

If you can't seem to get organized, set reminders on a calendar and highlight ultra-busy days in your planner. Prioritizing—not procrastinating—will make your must-dos more manageable.

TTG Secret No. 2:
She streamlines her sched

From homecoming committee to the river clean-up club, TTG seems to do it all. But she isn't joining any old club. She has selected a couple causes close to her heart and says oh-so-sorry to the rest.

Say you're all about curing cancer, but iffy about public speaking. Commit to that fundraiser for leukemia, but pass on debate club. You can give your all to what you are truly into—and stay sane, too.

TTG Secret No. 3:
She stresses less

Ever wonder how TTG stays so cool, even as things get superheated? She doesn't take herself too seriously. She knows that a little bit of LOL goes a long way, and she's right—studies show a sense of humor can relieve stress and lead to success.

So if your first day of dishwashing in the soup kitchen leaves ya covered head-to-toe in soapy water, laugh it off and go with the, um, flow.

TTG Secret No. 4:
She keeps a positive attitude

It may look like everything goes her way, but TTG has her share of not-so-great moments (hello, she's human!). The diff? She doesn't ditch her dreams when there's a bit of a setback.

Next time things don't go according to plan, take cues from TTG. Give yourself a little wallow time, then stop sulking and pursue your passion another way. OK, you didn't make the soccer squad. Why not coach a kids' team? You may not be the star, but you're still gonna shine.

TTG Secret No. 5:
She hollers for help

We have a news flash: TTG didn't rocket to star status by musclin' through every project solo. She likely has a major support network and asks for help when she needs it . . . and so should you.

Stumbling over a history assignment? Get tips from your teach after school. Swamped with swim practice? Ask your BFF to host the poster-painting sesh for the Blood Drive (you can return the favor later). Delegating tasks or sending out an SOS is totally OK—and one of the quickest ways to get (and stay) at the top.

TTG Secret No. 6:
She's got killer confidence

There's no hiding the fact that TTG knows what she wants and has the confidence to get there. Sounds a bit cheesy, we know, but believing in yourself really is the most important factor in achieving success. So even if you feel sorta shaky on the inside, self-confidence and a smile work wonders for your exterior. Just ask TTG—oh, wait, that's you!

Work It, Girl

We know you're not just dreaming about making the grades and getting the guy. A lot of you out there have much more long-term ideas in mind—namely, your dream job. Of course, that big J-O-B may be years away, but what's stopping ya from starting your career climb now? It all starts with snagging your first paid gig.

Know your limits

First things first. Before you make a list of dream jobs, check your state's child labor laws. In most states, you can't be officially employed until you're 14 (youthrules.dol.gov has details), which means that retail stores, traditional offices, and restaurants are probably out.

Another roadblock on the path to employment? Parents. Maybe they think your time is better spent at math camp. Maybe they aren't into driving you around. Maybe, yikes, they don't think you can handle the big, bad work world. Whatever their concerns, invite them to a sit-down. Calmly explain why you want a job. Address each issue, one-by-one ("I'll only plan to walk dogs at homes I can bike to.").

How do I pick the right activities?

It's about having fun and being involved, so start by checking out activities you liked in the past or things you know you have an interest in. Need ideas? Talk to a teacher or a guidance counselor who can give you a list of activities or tell you where to get one.

Once you decide on something, go to a meeting to gauge if it's truly for you. And, no, attending one meeting doesn't mean you have to join. If you like it, sign up. If not, just bounce. Some schools even host activities fairs so you can scope out the whole scene in an afternoon.

Can't find the right club for you? Start one! Ask a teacher, counselor, or school official to help you out. They can offer great advice on kick-starting your club and, that way, you'll be backed by the school so everything is legit.

Once you know your limits, list your possibilities. Cater to your interests and skills, but be open-minded. Love art but too young to man the register at the art supply store (and you were so looking forward to that employee discount!)? Instead, find out who needs help painting their dining room or stenciling the nursery (start with your own family to prove your skills, and spread out from there). See, you can put your art smarts to good use!

Be marketable

Set yourself apart by showing that you take your job seriously. For example, if working with children is your thing, take a babysitting class at a local YMCA or hospital. It'll make you stand out when you apply for that camp counselor position. Also, compile a list of references to hand to your potential client or employer. Impress much?

Get the word out

Ever hear that it's who you know that really matters? When it comes to jobs, it's often true. So work those connections. Do your parents or their friends need someone to handle the filing backlog at the office? Think your pal who already has a paper-delivery gig can hook you up? Let everyone know you're on the employment prowl.

If you're trying to start your own biz, advertise yourself and your services—word of mouth is key. For safety, limit yourself to people you and your family know. Then, they can refer you to future customers.

Meet and greet

Whether you've applied to the town's ice cream shop or have prospective babysitting clients, at some point you're going to have

81

to meet potential employers. You don't have to break out a business suit, but do look pulled-together and professional. It may be summer, but leave the short shorts, flip-flops, and tanks at home.

Prior to the job interview, jot down a list of questions you think you'll be asked, like "Why do you want to work here?" and "What do you have to offer?" Practice the answers with an older sib or parent. That way, no surprises.

After the big meeting is over *(phew!)*, send a follow-up e-mail or note thanking the interviewer for her time. If a week goes by and you still haven't heard, call to check the status of the position, and express your continued interest.

After that, if you don't hear anything, let it go. You're not gonna get every job you apply for, no matter how fab you are.

Startin' out

So you got the job. Yay! Now you just have to figure out your pay, hours, responsibilities . . . and, oh, yeah, how long until you can afford that killer bag! Go ahead and splurge on something you've been dying to buy with that first paycheck or two. But then, start putting at least half of the money away for a rainy day. It's never too soon to save for that future vacay, car, cell phone . . . And be proud of yourself, too. Between juggling work, friends, family, and activities, you are one together chica!

Jobs that won't feel like work!
(And rates that won't break the bank!)

✳ Computer lessons

Playing on your laptop is no big deal, but lots of adults could use a helping hand.
Perfect if you love: computers and are good at explaining things.
Skip it if you hate: a million questions or think a mouse is a rodent.
Pay day: $10 per hour and up.

✳ Mother's helper

From scrapbooking piles of pics to chores around the house, you pick up the slack for busy moms.
Perfect if you love: creativity and lots of variety.
Skip it if you hate: the unknown—your schedule, pay, and tasks will change daily.
Pay day: $5-10 per hour.

✳ Babysitting

Keeping kids safe and sound.
Perfect if you love: children, obviously, and jobs that'll keep you on your toes.
Skip it if you hate: major responsibility, being alone in a house at night, or dealing with overbearing parents.
Pay day: $7 per hour and up.

✳ Kiddie party planner

Put together birthday parties for tykes.
Perfect if you love: organizing big projects and being super-imaginative.
Skip it if you hate: clowns, balloon animals, and brats hopped up on sugar.
Pay day: $50 and up per party.

✳ Pet sitting and house watching

Summers are prime vacay time, so pups and homes need to be patrolled.

Perfect if you love: furry friends and making your own schedule.

Skip it if you hate: dog poop and working every day multiple times, without fail.

Pay day: $25 and up per job.

✳ Lawn care

Anything from mowing lawns to weeding gardens.

Perfect if you love: being outside and getting a workout while you work.

Skip it if you hate: bugs, dirt, and sweat. And just say no if you get sunburned easily.

Pay day: $15 and up per job.

The Bottom Line . . .

It's an awesome thing to chase your dreams—and even more amazing when you finally nab 'em. But just keep in mind that most goals take a lot of work—and time—before you see results. And, of course, there may be a setback or two along the way. Best way to handle any hiccups? Go easy on yourself and keep trying. Stay determined, remind yourself of why you want what you're after, and go for it again. Each day is a new one, and it's never too late for a fresh start!

Pretty Amazing

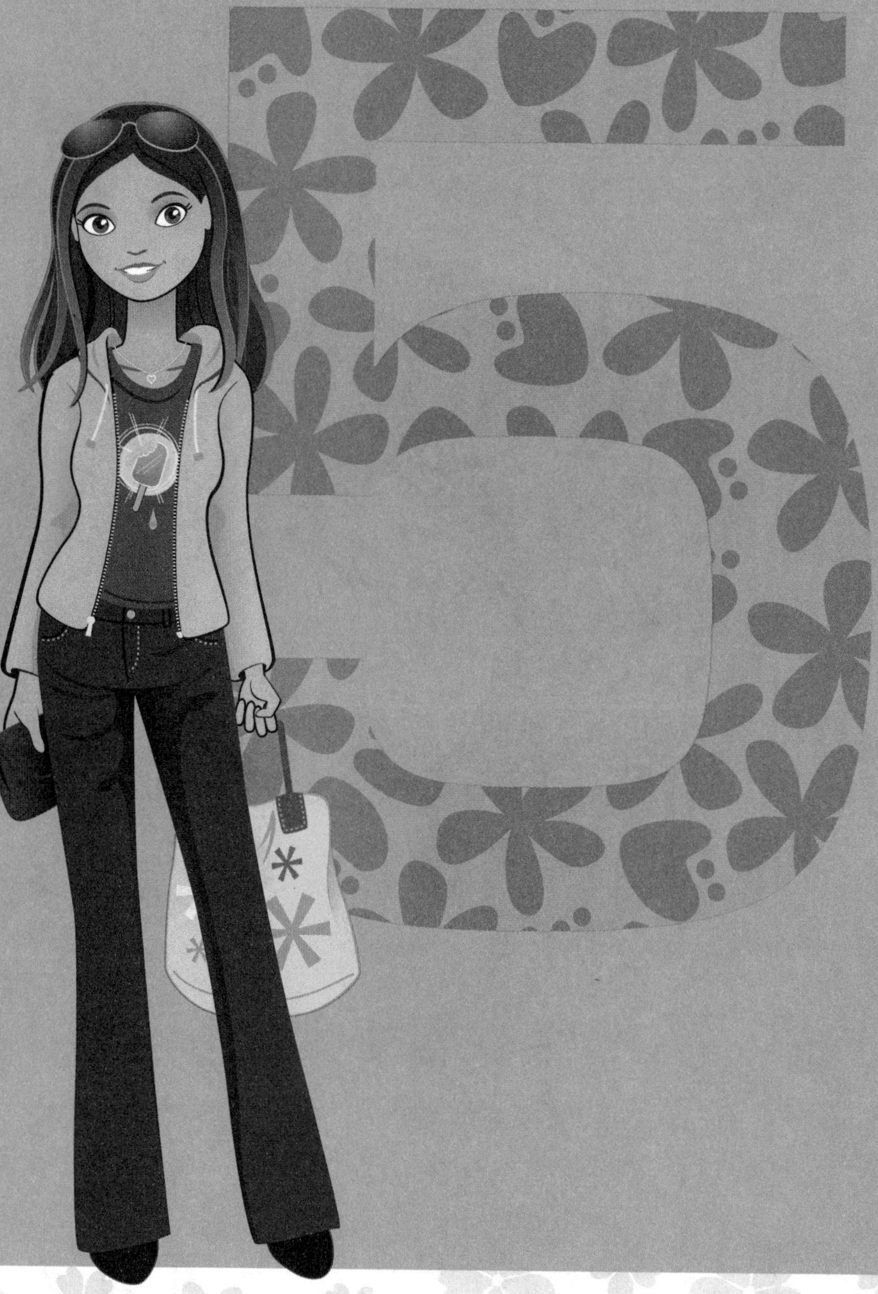

You just caught a glimpse of yourself in the mirror and aren't quite likin' what you see: Frizz doesn't even *begin* to describe what's going on with your hair, there's a ginormous zit on your nose, and you're barely fitting into your skinny jeans. *Ugh!*

Not quite BFFs with your bod? **You're not alone.** Most girls wage war on their bodies—and their looks— almost on a daily basis. But just because **your body's not doing what you want** it to doesn't mean you have to surrender to it by hiding under a hat til that zit fades away. You can **still be a confident** chica! How, you ask? Just read on, because we have everything you need to know about looking fab—and feeling *fierce!*

Confidence Comes First

Sure, your looks may be a huge concern for you right now. That's totally normal. But we've got some news for ya: Making a good impression on others isn't all about your looks. Instead, it's about coming across as super-confident and having that special sparkle that radiates from within.

So how do you shine even when you're not feeling your prettiest? We've got five no-fail tips for putting your best self forward—no matter what's going on with your hair these days.

Give Yourself a Hand

As if you needed another excuse to get a mani, here's one more: Your hands are one of the first things people notice about you. So, the prettier your paws are, the neater and more organized you'll seem.

But it's not just about glossy topcoat—it's *how you use your hands* that'll send the right (or wrong) signals. Case in point: Moving your hands around a lot can make you seem nervous. So slow down, and pay attention to any bad habits you have (twirling your hair and cracking your knuckles are major no-nos). Just make sure ya don't let the hands get too listless and limp. Gently animated movements (just say no to robot arms!) convey confidence.

The Eyes Have It

Maintaining great eye contact is one of the easiest ways to win someone over. Thing is, holding that gaze can feel a tad weird (you don't want to stare people down, obviously). Here's how to do it right: Practice *holding eye contact* in the mirror for ten seconds. Sounds silly, but it works. Now, when you meet with a mom about a potential sitting gig, focus on her face for that same ten-second period, then glance around thoughtfully, and look back at her. This will make you appear focused on the talk you're having, yet positively engaged with the world around you—a really appealing combo.

Push the Positive

Everyone enjoys being told they're awesome—and will most likely pay close attention to the person throwing compliments their way. So don't hesitate to *offer some sweet, sincere words* ("Great catch at the game!"). That's not to say you need to go crazy with praise ("The way you hold that pencil is just awesome!") or put yourself down ("Wow, no way I could have ever done that.") in the process. False flattery and self-deprecation will come off like you're trying too hard, or, even worse—insecure. Just be that genuine, generous girl that you are.

Find Common Ground

Here's a shocker: People relate better to those who seem just like them. Trying to click with a classmate? Pick out a subject to chat about that shows similarities. Let's say Sammy, a new girl you think *you might want to be friends* with, mentions she's really into making clothes. There's your chance to tell her you recently started using your mom's old Singer for fun. Can't find something totally in common? *Try a general topic* like the wacky weather or what might happen on the next season of a hot TV show. Keep the convo flowing and you'll come off as fab—not forgettable.

Ace an Excellent Exit

Think you've made a spectacular splash? Here's a parting shot you might not expect: Always leave 'em wanting more. At the end of your first encounter, *firm up any plans you've made* ("OK, I look forward to getting your call later this week and setting up some nights to babysit.") or sum up what you chatted about ("It's so cool that we both love sewing. *I'll text you* the next time I go fabric shopping!"). Then make a smooth exit by simply saying, "It was great to meet you, I'll talk to you later," and walk away. It's this kind of savvy confidence that can help ya secure your place in someone's mind for a very long time.

Flaunt What You've Got!

So once you've *got your confidence* cookin' from within, it's time to dress to impress! Clothes do not necessarily make the girl, but they can make ya look pretty fine if you've got the right looks going on. But don't feel like you have to conform to the latest trends or look exactly like your buds to turn heads. You should *find your very own fashion vibe* by wearing the clothes you're happiest in—and make you look your absolute best.

The first step to doing this is to *embrace your figure*—and all of its so-called flaws. Because whether you think you're too skinny or too curvy, too short or too tall, there's really no point in spending any more seconds wishing you had a different shape. Almost always, you can't do much about the body you were born with, and besides, we bet you're gorgeous just the way you are!

Of course, *pickin' the perfect looks* can be slightly less than a party. But we're here to make finding that fantastic outfit *waaay* easier. Here's a guide to selecting styles that'll flatter your body type. Stick to these tips next time ya go shopping, then get ready to flaunt!

Your Bod: Curvy 'N' Cute

● **When shopping for . . . Pants**

Look for: High-waisted boot cuts that keep the focus on a tiny waist. Pair with a tied shirt to play up curves.

Pass by: Low-slung pants that will draw attention to your hips.

● **When shopping for . . . Jeans**

Look for: Styles that show off your shape—not hide it! Flared or trouser jeans in dark washes work great, as do lower-rise waists. Just make sure the waistband doesn't cut in.

Pass by: Any cut that's too tight or adds extra curves, like skinny jeans. And skip funky stitching, washing, or detailing on the back pockets—you've got natural embellishments!

When shopping for . . . Shorts

Look for: Longer walking shorts that graze just above the knee and cute colors, skinny stripes, and girly plaids.
Pass by: Barely-there pairs or skinny styles that seriously taper.

When shopping for . . . Skirts

Look for: Retro pencil skirts. They show off your tiny waist! Find slightly longer hems (they'll lengthen lines) and go for a wide waistband.
Pass by: Shapeless skirts. The extra material will only add inches.

When shopping for . . . Dresses

Look for: Dresses that nip in the middle and have a bit of poof in the skirt. Tops with structure add to the bust if ya need it!
Pass by: Shift dresses (or any number that's straight up 'n' down). They won't do anything to show off your cute curves!

When shopping for . . . Bathing Suits

Look for: A knockout suit to show off those curves. Got a tiny waist? Choose a bikini with the same all-over color or print. Wider on top? Draw the eye upward by enhancing bust and shoulders with a halter top.
Pass by: Any details or cuts that'll draw more attention to your bottom half. So skip belts, ruffles, and brightly-patterned prints.

Your Bod:
Petite 'N' Sweet

⬢ **When shopping for . . . Pants**

Look for: Pants that sit at your waist. They'll lengthen legs. Pair with a blazer to define your shape.
Pass by: Pairs that hit at your hips. They shrink legs!

⬢ **When shopping for . . . Shorts**

Look for: Cute cuts that make legs look longer. Shorter inseams work well on smaller girls. Itty-bitty booty shorts are always a no-go, though.
Pass by: Don't box yourself in with oversize Bermudas.

⬢ **When shopping for . . . Skirts**

Look for: Fun minis that won't overwhelm your small shape. Pleats or stretchy fabric highlight cute curves.
Pass by: Long skirts. You'll drown in all that fabric!

When shopping for . . . Dresses

Look for: A skirt with cool cut-outs or a way-high waist—they'll add inches to your legs.

Pass by: Any dress that's just too long. Lots of length may make you look shorter.

When shopping for . . . Sweaters

Look for: Anything that's cropped or structured. You can also rock a slim cardi that works as a groovy dress.

Pass by: Bulky numbers that overwhelm.

When shopping for . . . Jeans

Look for: Pants that create *looong* lines. Higher waists (no higher than the belly-button, please!) are perfect to create the illusion of height. Straight legs, teeny flares, and skinny jeans all work to give your gams length.

Pass by: Bellbottoms and baggy jeans. Just like long dresses, bigger- and longer-cut jeans will make ya appear even more petite.

When shopping for . . . Bathing Suits

Look for: Bikini bottoms that sit lower on your waist to create the illusion of a longer torso. Vertical stripes or a one-piece with an empire waist will also make you look taller.

Pass by: Bikinis with bottoms cut too high and horizontal lines.

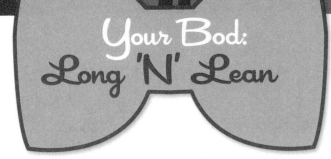

Your Bod: Long 'N' Lean

● When shopping for . . . Pants

Look for: Flared trousers and loads of layers (like a vest and bomber jacket) to add feminine flare.

Pass by: Skinny pants—they turn ya into a slip of a girl.

● When shopping for . . . Jeans

Look for: Fits that create curves. Try jeans that accentuate the hips (when bunched up at the bottom they trick the eye into seeing a wider calf.) Extra-wide legs work well with your height and create a rounder body shape

Pass by: Any jeans that aren't actually long enough for ya. Lotsa online versions of your mall faves have longer pants. So log on and snap them up.

● When shopping for . . . Shorts

Look for: Shorts that hit at the mid-thigh or lower. Go for DIY denim shorts: Snip 'em out to suit long legs.

Pass by: Too-short shorts can look scandalous on girlies with gams.

● When shopping for . . . Skirts

Look for: A fuller skirt with prints or pleats. It helps add feminine shape to a straight up 'n' down bod. Pretty prints help fake curves.

Pass by: Floor-length peasant skirts. It'll look like a tablecloth!

When shopping for . . . Dresses

Look for: Romantic ruffles or pretty prints to add the illusion of curves. Great detailing up top and longer hemlines also look good on taller girls.

Pass by: A too-simple, one-color dress. You want to add *oomph!* Avoid anything that's too-too short and snoozer skirts (aka, dresses that lack pleating, ruffles, or anything that's great and girly).

When shopping for . . . Sweaters

Look for: A short-sleeved turtleneck with pleating that helps create more curves up top. Or try sweaters with awesome accents, like bows.

Pass by: Thick knits that will flatten out the body.

When shopping for . . . Bathing Suits

Look for: Bold prints or horizontal stripes, which will undoubtedly create a wider look and add something in your chest and butt. Ruffles and frills also work to fill out a narrow figure.

Pass by: Dark colors, boy shorts, and bandeau tops. They just cut off curves, not create 'em.

The Complete Package

So now that you've got the clothes thing down, what about the rest of ya? Like fashion, *beauty is ultra-important* to creating the most amazing you, but sometimes it seems like your hair and skin are totally working against ya. Plus, figuring out *how to wear your hair*—or how much makeup to wear—can be pretty confusing, too.

Ask the Experts!

Your best source of advice for hair and makeup? Your *mom, girlfriends,* or better yet, the friendly woman behind the makeup counter at a department store or at that trendy new salon.

Makeup experts can teach you everything from how to

find your right shade and prevent breakouts, to how to apply your makeup—even how to remove it, too. Plus, if you want to go for a "natural" look, the experts are the ones who can give you an *FYI and all the right products.*

When it comes to your hair, a professional stylist can take a look at the shape of your face and the texture of your tresses, and suggest a look that'll work for you. Say you've got corkscrew curls. Well, that chic, sleek bob you spotted on your fave model isn't really going to happen with your hair. See what your stylist suggests instead, and we bet you'll end up loving your locks.

Five super-speedy tricks to get you gorgeous!

Forget Foundation
There's no need to slather foundation on your gorge face every A.M. Not only does it take forever, but it can make you look older. Instead, use a small amount of concealer to cover up blemishes and apply a tinted moisturizer over it. Let your natural beauty shine through.

Stick to the Essentials
Forget putting on a full face of makeup. Instead, apply two coats of black mascara for a wide-eyed look and a swipe of pink gloss. You'll look pretty and polished, with zero effort.

Pump up that Pony
A ponytail with volume is totally rockin' (and not a bit boring). Backcomb strands at the crown of your head with a small brush. Gather all of your hair into a sky-high pony. Add a cool elastic, and you're set.

Zap Drying Time
Blow-drying your hair can take forever and a day. When you're in a hurry, focus on the T-zone only (around your part and hairline). If it's too cold to go out with damp hair, use a dry shampoo to refresh locks.

Get Lippy
Make your lipstick work double (or triple) duty. Apply a couple of dabs on your cheeks and blend like crazy for a makeshift blush. Or use your fingers to smudge some on your lids as a girly eye shadow. Just make sure to blend, blend, blend, and add mascara.

99

Pretty is YOU

No matter your makeup routine or how darling your 'do, the most beautiful thing about you is, well, YOU! So remember **not to overdo it.** While foundation and concealer can be a great way to cover up zits and even out skin, don't cake it on.

Also unnecessary? Drawing on too-heavy liner to make your peepers stand out (a plain ol' swipe or two should do the trick) or globbing on hot pink lipstick (when a pretty gloss gives ya a better effect!).

Same goes for your hair—*don't spend too much time* messing around with the straightener, the curling iron, or piling on the products. For special occasions, feel free do it up, but if you're just going to school, remember that *your natural look is lovely.* After all, we are all beautiful in our own unique way and there's no reason to hide behind tons of makeup—or overdone hair.

The Bottom Line . . .

Your self-worth shouldn't be about the wrapping. Lots of other things are more important. If you don't have it goin' on inside, looking good on the outside isn't going cut it. Being friendly, outgoing, upbeat, kind, loyal, generous, and caring are qualities that make you attractive. So take that energy you waste trashing your looks and put it into being a better person. Not only will it increase your self-esteem and attract more friends, but it will put your body image in perspective as just one part of *Totally Irreplaceable and Amazing You.*

What's Your Style Vibe?

1. You're headed out for a day of shopping. What do you throw on that's casual, comfy, but still totally fresh?

A. An airy sundress with floral details. If it's chilly, you grab a jean jacket.

B. A loose-fitting printed top with head-to-toe beaded bling.

C. Black skinnies with a neon-yellow jacket. Add a studded cuff bracelet, and you're good to go!

D. Leggings and a basic white top with oversized shades.

2. What's on your shoe rack?

A. Several pairs of cowboy boots and a few pairs of high-heels for special occasions. Sometimes, you even rock it barefoot!

B. All flats all the time. Flip-flops, gladiators, ballet flats — you name it, you've got 'em!

C. Shoes are your fave! You have tons of platforms and pumps with kuh-razy colors and patterns.

D. You're mostly a strappy sandal girl and you've got 'em in all shapes and heights!

3. It's dance time! The dress code is formal and you really want to look fab to impress your crush . . . what do you wear?

A. A flirty cocktail dress with ruffled trim or one shoulder.
B. Something with soft and pretty details, like lace or bold embellishments.
C. A stand-out-in-the-crowd colored dress with gold accessories all over.
D. A bubble dress with a skinny belt at your waist.

4. What's one thing in your closet that you absolutely can't live without?

A. Cowboy boots, duh.
B. Your oversized bag.
C. Funkadelic shades.
D. Headbands.

5. If you had $1,000 to buy just one item of clothing or an accessory, what would you splurge on?

A. A to-the-floor gown in a flowy, silky material that makes you feel like you're floating.
B. An amazing piece of vintage jewelry, like a pendant encrusted in precious stones.
C. A super-hot leather jacket. Even better if it has funky details like zippers!
D. An adorable leather handbag. Pretty and practical.

Now tally up your answers and figure out your fashion match!

Mostly A's: COUNTRY GIRL

While sportin' beautiful, fab frocks, you always manage to keep it just a touch country. Who else can rock totally hip cowboy boots with a sequined cocktail dress? You, obviously! You love to play the girly girl with ruffles, but look totally flirty femme rockin' a tee, too.

Mostly B's: VINTAGE VIXEN

You're a total boho babe both who's in love with eclectic styles and vintage-inspired pieces, and you never cease to surprise others with your originality. You love pulling together (and totally rocking) outfits that no one else would think of.

Mostly C's: ROCKER CHICK

You'd never be caught dead donning a safe, "cute" dress—you like to mix it up and bring the heat wherever you go. Always opting to turn heads, you choose pieces with a distinct rocker edge while still looking oh-so glam. Good for you for having the courage to embody the essence of edgy chic!

Mostly D's: CLASSIC CHICA

It's safe to say that your style is totally classic—and totally cute. You love taking simple pieces from the day and pairing them with fab accessories for night! It's the small details that make your outfits stand out in a big way.

A Better You
(From the Inside Out)

6

Surely, there are things in life that you want so bad, you can almost taste 'em: A 4.0 GPA. A BF. A spot on the varsity volleyball team. So what's stopping you from going and getting them?

You might be **spending too much time** listening to that little voice inside ya saying that you're just not smart enough, or pretty enough, or athletic enough. That's just your **self-doubt talking,** and it's all a bunch of hooey!

It's time to transform the way you think about yourself, and here's all you need to know about dropping those doubts, **tackling those fears,** and diving headfirst into the amazing life you're meant to be living!

Be Fearless

Your life is packed with so many opportunities: cute new guys to scope, major extracurriculars to pick up, and tons of fun adventures with your buds. But, truth is, all those opps **can be overwhelming** and even scary sometimes. Whether you're afraid of your first-ever varsity tryouts or can't get up the guts to go out for the school play, we've got tips to get rid of those fears—fast!

Scary sitch:

You really want to star in the fall musical. And even though you're an awesome actor, you're **suddenly doubting** your dancing and singing moves for tomorrow's auditions.

Fear Not:

Sure, you may not be able to sing like a superstar or nail tricky dance steps—yet. But that doesn't mean you don't deserve a shot at the lead role. To kick up your confidence, make a "To Be . . . (in the musical, in this case)" list by writing out all of the traits you need in order to reach your goal. So if it's that role you're after, **write down what you've got** (great stage presence, acting experience) and what you still need to work on (pitchy probs, dance moves).

For an extra confidence kick, flash back to previous accomplishments (like when you brought your fam to tears last year while singing "Silent Night" to them over the holidays) or past fears you've conquered (remember when you were scared of the monsters under your bed? Pretty LOL-worthy now, right?). Then, *get working* on your not-so-strong skills—stat. After all, your fears shouldn't keep you from all the fab things you can accomplish.

Scary sitch:

Your Current Affairs teach just assigned a ginormous presentation on the state of the economy—and *you're sweatin'* speaking in front of the entire class.

Fear Not:

To truly get beyond this fear, you've gotta *confront it head-on* and expose yourself to scary stuff, like public speaking, bit by bit. A drama class may help you face your fears, but simply practicing for your parents, your cats, your friends, or any audience you can scrounge up will help ya get perfectly prepped for your presentation, too.

Scary sitch:

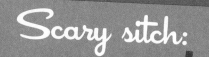

Twenty minutes til the start of your **state championship** cross country race and you're ready to run all right—all the way home.

Fear Not:

Believe us, even the most amazing athletes are nervous before a big race or match. There's just something about **competition that brings those what-ifs** (What if I get a cramp? What if my goggles fall off? What if I don't serve well?) crashing into your conscience, leaving ya shaking in your spikes.

The key to stopping yourself from getting psyched out? Close your eyes and envision what you want to have happen. This trick has helped tame the nerves of many professional athletes because it **helps you relax** and silence those very loud fears. So next time you're getting ready to race or face a challenge, take a quick look in your mental crystal ball and spy yourself kicking butt on the field, turning in your best time, or winning the game. Now that you've seen yourself succeed, it's time to take action.

Scary sitch:

You're starting a **new school** this year and are freaking about finding a new crew of friends.

Fear Not:

It's hard starting school solo, but being the new girl definitely has its privileges. For starters, you're going to be ten times **more interesting** to your classmates than the same ol' students they've been going to school with since first grade. (So there's a perk right there!)

Plus, there's bound to be one outgoing girl or guy who'll go out of their way to say hey. Ask that friendly face to show you around the school or clue you in on any shortcuts or tricks to traveling the halls (you can always ask a teacher for help, too). As for fitting in, the best way to carve a niche for yourself is to **join a club** or sport right off the bat. Finally, just be yourself—and be patient—and your new school will feel like home before ya know it.

Scary sitch:

The big dance is almost here. You're dreaming of dancing with *class cutie* Jake. If you could only ask him. . . .

Fear Not:

Sure, it would be wonderful if Jake swept ya off your feet with an invite fit for a fairy tale. But sometimes you need to **create your own** happy ending—whether it's a date to a dance or another major moment. So if you're itchin' to ask him out, just do it already!

Make sure he's def date-free, then grab him after math class or strike up a casual convo on your way to the caf. When there's a lapse in the chatter, take a deep breath then toss in your big Q (a simple, "Any chance you want to go to the dance with me?" is clear but casual). If he's into it, he'll be happy you made the first move. And if he turns you down? Well, you've gotta give yourself props for putting yourself out there . . . lots of girls wouldn't be so bold.

If things don't work out . . .

So let's say you faced your fears and things still didn't go quite as planned. Just remember that, sometimes, the outcome may not be just what you were hoping for. What to do next? Acknowledge your disappointment, dust yourself off, and make a new action plan. If you didn't win the class prez election, sign up for the eco club. Got cut from volleyball? Maybe the soccer league needs a few more players. Who knows, your life might start soaring in a totally new, more positive direction. And that's reason enough to celebrate.

Upping Your Oomph

So you're ready to face your fears and conquer every challenge that comes your way. Now we just need to make sure you've got the energy to do all that! Because if you're tired, you definitely can't tackle those tasks. And between school, homework, and everything else in your life, it's no wonder you're feeling so fried. But we're here to help ya banish the blahs with super-simple ways to get your *oomph* back—no Red Bull needed!

Lighten your lunch

You're running late for the bus, so you skip breakfast—and by the time lunch period rolls around, you're ready to stuff yourself silly. Sound familiar? But gorging at lunch can cause a major midday crash. Make sure you're *eating in regular intervals*, like something small every three or four hours. That includes breakfast, no matter how rushed you are in the A.M.

Move it!

Sure, a five-mile run might wear you out. But a little exercise can wake you up. So the next time you roll in from school and feel so pooped you just wanna plop, get your blood pumping for a few minutes. *Try walking* around the block, doing push-ups, or charging up a few flights of stairs. Then you'll be ready to tackle your next task.

Just breathe

You really have no choice on this one. But *how you breathe affects your energy.* The more oxygen you have flowing through your body, the more alert you feel. When you're stressed, your breathing becomes shallow—sapping your strength. Next time you want to hide under the covers, pause and take some *deeeeeeep* breaths. Or belt out your favorite tune—singing forces you to breathe more deeply.

Take a whiff

Hooked on lip balm and bath goodies? Use it to your advantage. Aromatherapy experts say certain smells— like citrus, cinnamon, rosemary, lemon, and mint— *perk you up.* Try an orange-scented shower gel in the morning, slick on peppermint lip gloss, or slather on some lemon-scented lotion. You can even choose a perfume that'll energize you every time you get a whiff.

Snack smart

When you're bushed, your body craves extra fuel. And while it's tempting to reach for a candy bar, you'll nod off again in an hour. Instead, go for snacks that *pack protein and fiber* (think nuts, string cheese, or yogurt), which will give ya a long-term energy boost instead of a quick buzz.

There's a reason baseball games always have a seventh-inning stretch—sitting still for too long can slow your circulation, which makes you drowsy. Like exercise, stretching gets your blood flowing, and it's way easier to pull off during a boring history class. Try this simple twist to *stretch your back* muscles:  Put your right hand on your desk and your left hand on your chair, then twist your torso to the left. Switch sides and repeat.

Get your ZZZ's

Face it—you're less likely to nod off in class if you actually got eight hours of shut-eye the night before. But does that ever happen? Between homework, *after-school* stuff, and your social life, you're lucky if you doze off before midnight. A recent study found that half of teens don't get enough sleep! But getting eight hours will keep you from drooling on your desk the next day. Besides, when it comes to stay-awake-during-geometry secrets, it doesn't get much simpler than plain old snoozing at night.

Drink Up

If you're feeling more sluggish than usual, you may be dehydrated—but don't *quench your thirst* with soda or coffee. Even though both give you an insta-buzz, you're better off hitting the water fountain. Not a fan of plain ol' H2O? Go for flavored water or tea—just keep it unsweetened and not strong.

Can't doze off, sleepyhead?

It's hard to squeeze in enough sleep—especially when your brain is buzzing with the day's drama. Make the most of bedtime. . . .

• Work out earlier. Since exercise is an energy booster, aim to finish your workout a few hours before you go to bed.

• Clear the clutter. It's hard to unwind when you've got textbooks and to-do lists piled all over the place.

• Get into a routine. Every night, take a hot bath or turn on your fave playlist—it'll signal to your brain that it's time to power down.

Finding Your Inner Strength

So now that you're taking care of that bod, it's time to get your inner strength in check. And that starts with becoming *super*. Nope, we're not talking about acquiring mega-strength or being able to swoop from skyscrapers like Spidey. This is about summoning the Supergirl inside of you—you know, the one who's smart, confident, and strong enough to stay grounded throughout all of life's loops. Good news: Every girl's got an inner heroine waiting to jump out. Here's how to find yours!

Be selfish (in a good way)

Becoming super requires a lot of attention on, well, you. And between pleasing your pals and doing favors for your fam, chances are you don't always put your needs first. But in order to reach your true, incredible potential, you have to prioritize in a personal way.

Now, this doesn't mean barking "I'm busy!" the next time your bro asks you to walk the dog, but it does mean curbin' the urge to drop everything and bend yourself like a soft pretzel.

One way to *maximize your Me Time?* Carve out an hour or two when you can do something completely personal— and productive (say, practicing tunes on your guitar or finally putting together that scrapbook from summer camp). Make an ironclad rule that *you won't let anyone interrupt* you while you're enjoying this activity. Turn off the cell, shut down the laptop, and tell your friends and fam they can bug ya again in an hour.

Not only will this make ya feel good for accomplishing something mega, but you'll see how empowering it can be when you place your interests just as high on your list as you do for others in your life.

Discover your superpower

Superman has X-ray vision. Wonder Woman can fly. The Hulk has superhuman strength. So what've you got? Are you really disciplined and consistent? Do you *smartly strategize* a sitch before making any moves? Are you willing to work longer and harder than anybody else?

Whatever your talent may be, it's important to be aware of your own unique strengths so you can use 'em to your advantage. Say you're gunning after a solo in show choir. How can you *play up your powers* to nab it? Stay after school to work on the number? Wow the crew with your very own creative twist on the tune? Use your power of persuasion to talk Teach into giving you the spot?

Knowing how to call upon your talents and powers will not only help ya stand out, but they'll make you brave enough to really go after what you want.

Cut the Clutter

Nope, not a reference to cleaning out your closet. Right now, it's all about surrounding yourself with *folks who help you feel incredible*—meaning it's time to let any toxic frenemies go. Do you have that one bud who's constantly crushing your aspirations into teeny-tiny pieces? And when you tell her, totally excited, about your plan to run for student council she snarks, "Um, only the popular kids win!"? Even if she softens her slam with a chuckle and a "JK!", you gotta realize that she's never going to be the kind of bud who wants you to succeed.

Of course, we're not saying you should drop your bad news bud like last week's leftovers. What to do instead? Get genuinely busy *pursuing your goal.* (Write that speech! Shake those hands! Make those campaign signs!) Inevitably, you won't have any time to hang and you'll naturally drift apart. The result? You'll be able to express your incredibleness in all its ragin' glory.

Look forward to failure

Every superhero faces tons of challenges—overcoming 'em is what makes them so, well, incredible. And roadblocks are gonna pop up for you, too, no doubt. Did you know, though, that you can actually use those disadvantages to power up your 'tude? It's all about retraining your brain to take setbacks in stride instead of letting them stifle your amazing self.

To start, cancel all pity parties when something goes wrong—especially when there's no one to blame but yourself. OK, so it really stinks when you blow something. But try not to bash yourself for your blunder. Review your decision-making process to see where you went wrong—and figure out a solid plan to avoid missteps in the future.

And when bigger issues pop up, like a botched audition or campaign defeat? Sure, it can be hard to dust yourself off after a disaster, but don't let it stop you from doing what you do—and trying again. Give yourself a 24-hour window to mope around, then get back out there ready to tackle whatever hurdle is placed in your path.

Take risks the right way

In order to reach ultra-incredible heights, you're gonna have to take a chance now and then. But facing too many challenges may lead ya to just crumble. So what's the secret to success? Learning to choose your risks the right way.

Say you've been *training really hard* for three upcoming indoor track meets—when, suddenly, your coach tries to persuade you to run an outdoor 5K. You love to race, but you know your muscles take forever to recover from a frigid run. And running the 5K may jeopardize your chances to do well at the meets you've been training for.

So what should ya do, Miss Incredible? Be practical—*stick to your plans,* and shred those indoor meets. Explain your reasons to your coach and use the fact that she had so much confidence in your talent as the praise—and energy—you'll need to achieve the goals most important to you.

In the end, reaching your top potential is just like a well-run race, anyway. You've gotta *have faith in yourself* to reach the finish line—and if you take the right steps steadily along the way, winning is really no sweat. Incredible, right? So are you!

The Bottom Line . . .

Just like freshening up that topcoat on your fingernails or switching out your makeup for the new season, it's good to give your mind a little makeover once in a while, too. We all need to clear the clutter in our brains—to banish those bad thoughts and negative 'tudes that have us ditching our dreams. So whenever you're feeling especially stressed or down, take a few minutes to think about what you want and how to get there. Didn't get that lead role the first time around? Come up with a new plan of action for the next round of auditions. Whatever you do, don't give up on something you really, really want. Why? Because anything is possible for an amazing girl like you!

1. Be Conscious of Your Conscience

It's that little voice inside that warns you when you're about to do something that would make your parents cringe. Pay attention to your gut even if it's not so much fun. It will not only save you from getting grounded, but a guilty conscience can bring on some sleepless nights. Hey, is being good really so bad?

2. Jump into a Project

Do whatever has you flexing your creative muscles. Knit, cook, paint, whatever! No pressure—just something fun to focus on, and when you finish your project, you'll spill over with pride and confidence in knowing you crafted such a cool creation.

3. Stop, Look, and Listen

Take a break, and go outside to clear your head. Things are happening outside your hectic life. Appreciate the little stuff, like the ladybugs that sunbathe on your windowsill—and even that math test won't feel like the end of the world.

4. Walk this Way

You can't always control what happens in your life, but you can control how you react. Before your face turns scarlet and steam blows from your ears, take a walk! Sometimes, the best way to relieve stress is to hit the pavement and take a breath of fresh air. Clear you mind, and pump up a positive vibe. Bonus: Walking is great exercise!

5. Lend a Hand

You've heard it a million times, but volunteering really is a great way to feel good inside! It's all about helping people because you want to, not because you have to. You'll meet new people, make a difference, and feel appreciated.

123

Are you the real you?

Do you mold yourself to fit in—or do you so not give a hoo-ha about what people think of you?

1. You score a wild new pair of platforms at the mall. When you show 'em to your BFF, though, she wrinkles up her nose and says, "Ick—what were you *thinking*?" What's your comeback?

A. "I should take them back. Good thing I saved the receipt."

B. "OK, I guess they are kinda fierce. I'll save 'em to wear to the Fall Ball."

C. "I love 'em! I'm gonna bust them out in homeroom first thing Monday morning."

2. Your crazy-cute crush promised to text you over the weekend, but you never heard from him. So what's your move?

A. You freak out. What did you do wrong?

B. You IM him to find out what's going on.

C. You just chill—maybe he got busy and forgot.

3. You hear your grandma chatting about you and your sibs. She calls your sis "the pretty one," your bro "the smart one," and you "the sweet one." Does this bother you even a little bit?

A. Uh, how about a lot. Obviously, everyone thinks you're hopelessly ugly and dopey.

B. Kinda. You think you look fine and sound pretty intelligent, but maybe you're all wrong about the way you come across to others.

C. Nope, no biggie. That's sweet she thinks you're sweet!

4. You get a funky, choppy bob you love. When you show it off to your BF, he yelps, "Aw! I liked your long hair!" Still diggin' the 'do?

A. Not one bit—you're getting extensions, pronto.

B. Yeah . . . but maybe you shouldn't have gone so short.

C. Of course! It's your hair. He'll get used to it.

5. The mean girl in your grade wrote in her blog that you're fat 'cause she saw you putting on size 10 jeans in the locker room. The first thought that pops into your head is . . .

A. "How can I lose five pounds quick?"

B. "That stung."

C. "Who cares what she blogs? I look great!"

6. It was your mom's b-day yesterday . . . and you blanked, not even remembering to get her a card. Today, when you apologized, she said, "Well, my feelings are pretty hurt, and I'm disappointed in you." You reply . . .

A. "You must think I'm the worst daughter in the entire world!"

B. "Great, now I feel really guilty."

C. "I hate to make you feel bad. Let's go out to lunch today, my treat."

Mostly A's

Camo Chica

You're a chameleon. You rely on others to tell you who you are, rather than recognizing your own fabulousness. It's time for you to learn to value your ideas, likes, and dislikes as valid. Start outwardly expressing your true feelings about things—you'll quickly see how good it feels to speak your mind for a change, and how cool your opinions really are.

Mostly B's

Gutsy Girl

You have sharp instincts when it comes to knowing who you are inside. Sometimes, though, sticky sitches might get you a bit flustered and second-guessing yourself. Nobody knows you better than . . . you, so when you've got a hunch about something, trust yourself enough to go with it. You're way too awesome to waste even a second letting others steer you the wrong way.

Mostly C's

Leadin' Lady

You truly don't care what other people think of you—you're oozing self-confidence, and you're never afraid to blaze your own trail. Just be sure you don't get so set in your own super-strong way of thinking that you diss or dismiss the way other people feel. Different thoughts and perspectives make life exciting, so respect where your buds are comin' from even if it's totally opposite your way.

Index

The advice girls are looking for about practically everything!

From breakouts to periods, and everything in between, this guide delivers the body basics to help you look and feel fabulous!

Max out on your best moments with advice on how to handle first day jitters, fights with friends, and more!

You can't avoid ALL drama! This guide will help you deal with guys, friends, family, and more!

From classes to cuties to curfews—and everything else—getting exactly what you want is way easier than you think.